The Tree of Life

A Biblical Study of Immortality & New Creation

The Tree of Life

A Biblical Study of Immortality & New Creation

PAUL SELLMAN

Outskirts Press, Inc.
Denver, Colorado

The Tree of Life
A Biblical Study of Immorality & New Creation

v2.0 r1.2

Outskirts Press, Inc.
http://www.outskirtspress.com

ISBN: 978-1-4327-6232-2

PRINTED IN THE UNITED STATES OF AMERICA

Dedication:

To the people at Monroe Covenant Church, who gave me the freedom as their pastor to go without fear where the Bible goes. They heard much of what I wrote here in lessons and sermons and we had a loving give and take over the ideas. Like most people, they were challenged by what I found in Scripture, but let me explore and contemplate. When I accepted the call to pastor them, I thought I was doing them a favor. Now that I have moved on, I see more clearly and realize that it was they who did me a favor by letting me lead them. They are the nicest and kindest church I have ever been a part of, and I will always be grateful for my time there.

And to LMP.
I need not say more.

Acknowledgments:

When writing about a deep and wide ranging subject as this book does, the claim for originality goes out the window. What I've written here is the result of years of study, innumerable conversations and reading the works of other people. All these sources come together in this place to make the case I am making in this study.

Having said that, I want to thank four people in particular:

First, I owe a lot to N.T. Wright and his writings. What I wrote in this book are my own conclusions, but his thinking and scholarship had a major impact on my ability to put things in order. I had the vast majority of pieces on the table, but from Rev. Wright, I gained the ability to organize these thoughts. This is not to imply his agreement or endorsement for my work here, but I am indebted to him.

Second, I am grateful to Jim Crouse for reading the manuscript in its earliest and unfinished form. His insights and comments made this a better work. Also, it was he who pointed out the arrow in the FedEx logo (see the introduction), and he wants everyone to know it. We were near Monterey, California riding our motorcycles, when he spotted it on a building. It took him about 10 minutes (and a paper and pen) to drive it home to me so that it finally became clear to my eyes. He still mocks me about this.

Third, I give special thanks to Joe Fleming, who also read the manuscript and made very important observations about my own contradictions, inconsistencies and grammar mistakes. I had to re-examine several portions because of his astute observations. Besides his help here, there are hundreds of hours of open honest discussion over Scripture, faith and theology, with complete freedom to think aloud without fear. We have the ability to openly disagree with brotherly love. Unfortunately, in my experience, this is too rare in Christian circles. Our conversations have made me a better thinker, and a better person.

Fourth, just when I thought my book was safely finished, my sister Arlys Ferrell got a hold of it. I was mortified when I saw how many corrections were flowing from her pen. I suspected that this was revenge for all the times she had to drag her little brother (me) to Candlestick Park to watch the Giants play. But in the end, this book is far, far better for her having worked it over. Thanks, R!

Finally, a special thank you to Ron & Donna Golden for their generous help in getting this book published. Not only that, Ron gave me a good deal on his motorcycle. Thanks, guys!

Contents

Introduction

How This Book Started

We don't want to die. Generally speaking, we don't like thinking about death, we don't like facing our mortality, and when seriously ill, we do what we can and spend great amounts of money to avoid death. I like what Woody Allen said: "I'm not afraid to die; I just don't want to be there when it happens."

If we don't avoid the subject entirely, we then find systems of thought to help us face death, in particular, religion. For millennia, around the world different cultures have formed belief systems to explain what happens when we die. All sorts of things kick in: the idea of immortality, other worlds, reincarnation, and so on.

I do not want to compare or criticize any of the systems

but rather, I want to focus on just one: Christianity and the Bible. In focusing on just this one belief system, it will by default imply the differences between Christian beliefs and others. However, the approach taken by this book will also point out the weaknesses of common Christian beliefs which in fact do not have Biblical support, even though they are considered mainstream points of view.

I began my faith journey holding to this particular set of beliefs, which goes as follows: humans are sinful creatures with immortal souls who need redemption. If we commit our lives to Christ, then we are saved. When we die, we then go to heaven for all eternity, and those who reject Christ spend all eternity being tormented in hell. This is standard Evangelical Christian thought. The point of this book is to demonstrate that much of this thinking is simply not Biblical, and therefore, it's incorrect.

As I said already, my faith journey began with holding exactly this belief. Then one day, I was reading my Bible and the question hit me: how come the Old Testament doesn't say much about dying and going to heaven? I didn't think it could be a new idea with the New Testament writers. I looked and looked and simply couldn't find anything said about the matter. Then it got worse. The more I thought about it, I realized that considering how central a place the notion has for Christians (and people in general), *the New Testament doesn't say much about dying and going to heaven, either.* Some of the apostle Paul's statements seem to say this, and I had been taught to see it, but when

I looked with a more discerning eye, I realized that much of what I had assumed to be Christian belief did not have good scriptural basis.

Problems With The Standard Ideas

The more I thought about it, the more problematic the situation became. I would often approach a passage and ask myself, "If I had not been told what the interpretation of this verse was, how would I interpret it?" Try it some time. You'll find that it can be an eye-opening experience. Soon, I had stumbled onto some considerable difficulties which needed resolving, such as:

- The Bible *nowhere* says that the soul is immortal. I have challenged audiences at times to name one verse that does, and nobody refutes it. In fact, the Bible flat out says that *only* God is immortal (1 Timothy 6:16).
- Repeatedly, the Bible refers to the deceased as asleep. Each of the kings of Judah and Israel are said to have "slept with his fathers" and Paul refers to the deceased as "asleep in Christ." If people die and go to heaven, this is really a strange way to describe a glorious existence with Jesus. We can imagine all sorts of ways that life with Jesus will be like: no aches and pains, no sorrow, sheer bliss and non-fattening chocolate all spring to mind. But the idea of sleeping does not convey a great and glorious communion with Him.

- If we die and go to heaven, why is there so much talk about resurrection? One of the things that will be seen in this study is that more is said about the resurrection of God's people than about the resurrection of Jesus. What would be the point of such a thing as resurrection if we are already in total bliss in heaven?
- The Old Testament, Jesus, and Paul all repeatedly made reference to a judgment day where the wicked are separated from the righteous. If we die and go to heaven, does that mean judgment day comes after we've been in heaven (or hell) for a while? What would be the point?

By now, you get my drift. There are key ideas repeatedly given in scripture that have to be ignored and eliminated in order to hold to the standard view which gets passed off as "Christian" theology. This book is my attempt to place everything back in what I consider to be the proper order of things. In so doing, we will find that the entirety of scripture will be included and restored, both Old and New Testaments.

The Biblical Framework Of History

In order to lay out this theology, I am going to use the lens that ancient Judaism used, and which was also used by Jesus and Paul as well. In American Evangelical Christianity, we've really gotten things tangled up with talk of dispensations, tribulation, millenniums, and so on. It's really much simpler than this, and this study will establish how clearly the Bible speaks to this subject. Here is the outline of all history as seen in scripture:

This Age / The Day of Yahweh / The Age to Come

If you doubt me, here is a quick study:

Matt 12:32 "Whoever speaks a word against the Son of Man, it shall be forgiven him; but whoever speaks against the Holy Spirit, it shall not be forgiven him, either in **this age** or in **the age to come**."

1 Cor 2:6-8 Yet we do speak wisdom among those who are mature; a wisdom, however, not of **this age** nor of the rulers of **this age**, who are passing away; but we speak God's wisdom in a mystery, the hidden wisdom which God predestined before the ages to our glory; the wisdom which none of the rulers of **this age** has understood; for if they had understood it they would not have crucified the Lord of glory;

Eph 1:20-22 ...which He brought about in Christ, when He raised Him from the dead and seated Him at His right hand in the heavenly places, far above all rule and authority and power and dominion, and every name that is named, not only **in this age** but also **in the one to come**.

"This Age" is the current state of affairs. From Adam and Eve's fall, to this very moment, we are living in This

Age. It is marred by sin, disease, oppression, and unending sorrow. We ask why things are the way they are and what went wrong?

"The Day of Yahweh" is the great dividing point between the two ages. I clearly point out in this study that the Day of the Lord is definitely not an old discarded relic of ancient Judaism; it is retained and *emphasized* by Paul and is the great hinge point of his theology. Simply put, the Day of the Lord is when the bad guys get punished, and God's people are delivered.

"The Age To Come" is the fulfillment of all that we wish God would do to make a better world. No more death, oppression and sorrow. Life is always good, non-stop, and everything works the way it's supposed to.

This may seem unbelievably simple, given the current trends in pop theology, but I will address it further down the road. The reason I raise this issue is because this is how this study will be laid out and organized: This Age, The Day of Yahweh, and The Age To Come. To use this framework, I believe, is to frame it in approximately the same way that Jesus and Paul would have done it. That's a big claim I know, but I think this study will bear this out.

Some Thoughts Before Beginning

This study will probably make you feel a bit disoriented because it challenges many of the assumptions that we are taught to believe in our churches. Having said that, I'd like to make a few comments:

First, this study will be Biblically based. I will provide plenty of information and background to support whatever assertions I make, and I will tackle some of the rough spots which challenge our thinking. In some cases, I will simply admit that I don't have a good answer for a question. Give this study a fair hearing, and I think you'll be surprised at how much scripture has been overlooked in popular Christian thinking.

Second, if this study seems like an overwhelming overturning of your beliefs, my own journey from traditional theology to this view took me years to make. I did not seek to have a new opinion; I simply kept finding new angles to consider and then went and re-read many passages that I took for granted and realized that they pointed in a different direction than I had been going.

Third, in many cases, I provide many verses to support a point, and in many cases, there are more than needed. I sincerely suggest that you read every reference I list, and you will see how thoroughly the Bible covers these ideas.

Fourth, everybody has their pet verse, or 'go to passage' when encountering this theology. I challenge you to consider the overall weight of the verses I refer to in this study. Roughly 200 passages are drawn upon in making my case. Consider the overall framework presented in the Bible before you dismiss it with two or three verses. I think you will find that 'the exceptions prove the rule'.

Finally, I'd like to offer an analogy before we begin. Have you ever noticed The FedEx logo on one of their trucks? There's an interesting story behind it. If you look carefully, you'll notice that between the 'E' and the 'x', that there is an arrow pointing to the right. This was deliberate in the logo design. I never noticed this arrow until recently, when my friend Jim pointed it out to me. Now when I look at a FedEx truck, I can't help but see it. It's everywhere!

It's the same with the theology presented in this book. If you give a fair reading to the Bible as I present it here, all of a sudden, you will see something different. Instead of the standard Christian theology as I presented it above, you will see the following: We live in *This Age,* which is marred by sin and death. We are mortal, mortal, mortal, and when we die, we really are dead, and nothing but dead. We *don't die and go to heaven; we lie in the ground!* Then, when Christ returns, the dead are raised, and along with the living, are judged before God on the *Day of the Lord.* Then, after sin and death are conquered, and the wicked destroyed, the *Age to Come* begins, and we then – and only then – are granted eternal life *via* the Tree of Life.

Because the Tree of Life is central to this theology which I present, I have named this book after it. The whole story that the scriptures tell, from Genesis to Revelation, is about life. I think you'll find this theology, this story, very refreshing once you get used to it.

Soli Deo Gloria!

Paul Sellman

May, 2010

Part One: This Age

In this section, we see how humankind was placed under the curse of death. This happened in the Garden of Eden, when Adam & Eve rebelled against God. Afterwards, a very clear statement about our mortality is given.

In this age, death is the power over us. Both the Old and New Testaments attest to our mortality and complete subjection to this power. In both testaments, all people are said to die, and to lie in a state of unconsciousness.

1. The Garden: Death & Our Lost Immortality
2. Sheol (Old Testament)
3. Hades (New Testament)
4. Asleep In Christ

1

The Garden: Death and Lost Immortality

The story is tragic, but offers hope. We are created by a loving God, provided for by Him, but then we rebel and lose everything we saw. This happens through a lie: the serpent tells Eve that God lied to her, that *she will not die* like He said, but instead, she will be like God. Check it out:

> ***Genesis 2:15-17*** *Then the LORD God took the man and put him into the garden of Eden to cultivate it and keep it. 16 The LORD God commanded the man, saying, "From any tree of the garden you may eat freely; 17 but from the tree of the knowledge of good and evil you shall not eat, <u>for in the day that you eat from it you will surely die</u>."*
>
> ***Genesis 3:1-6*** *Now the serpent was more crafty than any beast of the field which the LORD God had made. And he said to the woman, "Indeed, has God said, 'You shall not eat from any*

tree of the garden'?" 2 The woman said to the serpent, "From the fruit of the trees of the garden we may eat; 3 but from the fruit of the tree which is in the middle of the garden, God has said, 'You shall not eat from it or touch it, or you will die.'" 4 The serpent said to the woman, "You surely will not die! 5 "For God knows that in the day you eat from it your eyes will be opened, and you will be like God, knowing good and evil."

Genesis 3:22-24 *Then the LORD God said, "Behold the man has become like one of Us, knowing good and evil; and now, he might stretch out his hand, and take also from the* ***tree of life****, and eat, and live forever. – therefore, the LORD God sent him out from the garden of Eden, to cultivate the ground from which he was taken. So He drove the man out; and at the east of the garden of Eden He stationed the cherubim and the flaming sword which turned in every direction to guard the way to* ***the tree of life****.*

Having passed over some parts of the story, we can get to the nub of the situation. There are two particular trees in the Garden. One is the Tree of the Knowledge of Good & Evil, and the other is the Tree of Life. Adam & Eve are warned away from the Tree of Knowledge.

Interesting questions arise here: previous to the Fall, did Adam & Eve eat of the Tree of Life? Were Adam & Eve originally immortal? We aren't told one way or another. If they were immortal, it becomes clear later that they lost this. My guess (and it's only a guess) is that they had not eaten of the Tree of Life, because the result of doing so is immortality (3:22).

Having said that, there are several things that happen

in the story which we should notice. First of all, God says without any ambiguity, "eat this, and you will die." This usually gets interpreted as spiritual death, and this is true, but too often, 'death' gets redefined as meaning "to live forever in a different way." I think God actually was saying this: "You will die."

Obviously, this didn't take effect right away, for the story goes on and Adam and Eve go on to live very long lives, actually. But the curse did take effect: Adam and Eve eventually did die. And they weren't supposed to. They did not die that day, *but they most certainly did become mortal beings, if they weren't already..*

Second, the lie that the serpent told Eve was that she would not die. This was a half truth in a sense, for as we noted, she and Adam continued to live for a while, *but they died later. The serpent lied to them with a promise of immortality!* I find it highly ironic that in the name of Christian theology, many people hang on to the lie of the serpent and say that people are immortal. This is the great, great lie underlying all humanity.

Think of all the religions that have formed that teach and empower people to hold to a view that they will live forever. Pharaohs built pyramids in their quest for immortality. The belief in ghosts is a claim to immortality. When someone dies, the relatives gather and comfort themselves by saying "He/She is in a better place now…" But the warning from God was that we will die, and the lie from the serpent was that we shall have immortality.

Who are you going to believe?

Third, notice God's response. Now that His creatures have fallen, and now that they have shame, what happens? God cuts off their access to the Tree of Life. Why? The answer is given to us: *because if they eat of the tree of life, they will live forever.* The implication is clear: the Tree of Life represents immortality, and we didn't get to it. It couldn't be more plain: God removed the option for immortality from the table.

Most theologians say that this was done because humankind was now in a fallen, defiled state, and God didn't want them living forever in that condition. This is correct; however, they usually get it only half right. Most people go on to then say that we are still immortal. Once again, we believe the lie of the serpent over the warning of God. The fallout (pun intended) of Adam & Eve rebelling was that we fell from life to death.

There is one central point that I want to make in this chapter: *We are not immortal in any manner, shape or form.* God said that sin will cause death and He meant it. The serpent lied and said we will have immortality.

So why do we teach the standard Christian view? There are a couple of reasons. First, much of our theology is a hybrid of culture, philosophy and the Bible. Theoretically, Bible believing Christians use the Bible first and foremost above all other sources, but this often isn't the case. Very early in the church, the leaders were trying to make the Christian faith amenable to Greek philosophy. Some Greek philosophy schools believed that the human soul was immortal; however, this was not the Jewish way of looking at it. We will make this clear later. Along the way, Greek philosophy became part of our method of reading scripture, and we began to see things that aren't really there.

Second, I believe that we are intrinsically wired to live forever. Something lies within us from the very beginning that expects to live forever. Genesis says that we were created in the likeness of God, and part of that is a sense of the eternal. Throughout history, people have made statements like "I *know* that something inside me lives forever" or some such thing. It's understandable, because the idea of death is awful.

God's warning was clear: you will die. So here is a quick challenge: *name one single verse in the Bible that says the human soul is immortal*. There is none. I've heard people suggest that the Bible teaches about the immortal soul, but it simply isn't true. You cannot name a verse anywhere.

Quite the opposite, there are clear statements about our condition. In 1 Timothy 6:16, Paul says that God *alone* is immortal. What this *should* mean to us is that only God has immortality; instead, Christian theology often takes this verse to mean we all are immortal. I don't see how it could be any clearer. In 1:17, Paul refers to God as immortal, the implication being that all else is *mortal.*

In 1 Corinthians 15:18 where he is talking about the resurrection, Paul says that if there is no resurrection, then *those who have died have already perished.* Gone. No more. That is not the talk of someone who believes in an immortal soul. Furthermore, in the same chapter, Paul says that the "perishable must put on imperishability, and the mortal put on immortality." These statements usually get interpreted in a manner that reverses the truth they teach. Paul was not saying that our *mortal bodies* must put on immortality; he was saying that we are completely mortal, body and soul. If we were already immortal, we would not need to 'put on' immortality.

Throughout the Old Testament, there is a bleakness which the Christian writings don't have. Mortality casts a long shadow over the Hebrew scriptures. The reason is because immortality of the soul was not in their thinking. There are on occasions some glimmers of vague hope that God will do something redemptive in the afterlife, but generally speaking, for ancient Hebrews, someone's passing was the end of the story.

We have made mention of the Tree of Life. After Genesis 3:24, what happens to it? We do not see it again until Revelation 22.[1] The implication is staggering: the hope of immortality is not fulfilled until the final events described at the end of the Bible in a "new heavens and new earth."

If you want to believe that we are immortal beings, you have the right; but you simply cannot say that this is a Biblical belief. The rest of part one will come back to this point and reinforce it.

1 There are several references to a tree of life in Proverbs, but they are not specifically in reference to the one which was in the Garden of Eden.

2

Sheol: The Old Testament Abode of the Dead

Depending upon your translation, you may never see this word 'Sheol' in the Old Testament, but the concept is everywhere. Why don't you see it then? Because, taking the NIV as an example, they take 'Sheol' and translate it 'grave.' This does a disservice to the reader. It is a proper name, and by translating it as they do, it becomes neutralized.

In talking about the afterlife in the Old Testament, there are two basic ideas presented. First, most of the time, the expectation is that nothing happens after you die; it's just over. Second, there are occasional hints of another life after death, but where this happens, it is a vague hope rather than a clear statement. In this chapter, I will deal only with the first case, and I will address the Old Testament hope of afterlife in chapter 7.

We will now do a survey of Sheol in the Old Testament.

> ***Numbers 16:30*** *"But if the LORD brings about an entirely new thing and the ground opens its mouth and swallows them up with all that is theirs, and they descend alive into* ***Sheol****, then you will understand that these men have spurned the LORD."*

What we see here is pretty typical of the use of 'Sheol.' We are told the deceased go there, but not much information is given. When you read all the mentions of Sheol, you will find that they are not much different than what you see here: you are told someone went (or will go) there, but not much more.

> ***Job 14:13-15*** *"Oh that You would hide me in* ***Sheol****,*
> *That You would conceal me until Your wrath returns to You,*
> *That You would set a limit for me and remember me!*
> *14 "If a man dies, will he live again?*
> *All the days of my struggle I will wait until my change comes.*
> *15 "You will call, and I will answer You; You will long for the work of Your hands."*

In this passage, Job is tired of suffering and wants it to be over. He wishes to be hidden in Sheol. Why? Because there is no consciousness there, and he won't feel any pain any longer. In vs. 14, he asks a rhetorical question: "Will someone live again after they die?" The *implied* answer is that they will not. Job's comfort is not for a better life after this one, but the end of feeling his current pain.

> ***Job 17:13-16*** *"If I look for* ***Sheol*** *as my home, I make my bed in the darkness;*
>
> *14 If I call to the pit, 'You are my father'; To the worm, 'my mother and my sister';*
>
> *15 Where now is my hope? And who regards my hope?*
>
> *16 "Will it go down with me to* ***Sheol****? Shall we together go down into the dust?"*

As we saw in the previous passage of Job, there is the sense of finality regarding Sheol. Job assumes that Sheol will be the end of it all and that his body will be consumed by worms. In vs. 15, it is clear that hope is at an end. He and his hope are finished off for good.

> ***Psalm 6:5*** *For there is no mention of You in death; In* ***Sheol*** *who will give You thanks?*

You can't say it more clearly than this: nothing happens in Sheol. There is no consciousness. Death and Sheol are partners in non-existence.

> ***Psalm 49:14-15*** *As sheep they are appointed for* ***Sheol;*** *Death shall be their shepherd;*
>
> *And the upright shall rule over them in the morning,*
>
> *And their form shall be for Sheol to consume so that they have no habitation.*
>
> *15 But God will redeem my soul from the power of* ***Sheol,*** *For He will receive me. Selah.*

Once again, Sheol is the place of death and of being consumed by decay. This passage also touches upon a hope of resurrection, to be covered in chapter 7. The phrase "And the upright shall rule over them in the morning" may refer to the living who survive the wicked or to a form of resurrection.

***Proverbs 27:20 Sheol** and **Abaddon** are never satisfied, nor are the eyes of man ever satisfied.*

Once again, Sheol (and Abaddon) are rendered as a place of decay and being consumed. The proverb's intent is to lament a person's insatiability with things. We always want more and more, no matter how much we take. No promise of future life can be inferred by this proverb, but rather, it maintains the Old Testament motif of no future.

***Proverbs 30:15-16** There are three things that will not be satisfied, four that will not say, "Enough": 16 **Sheol,** and the barren womb, Earth that is never satisfied with water, And fire that never says, "Enough."*

Like the proverb before it, once again the image is about our natural insatiability. A barren womb always longs to be filled; earth always wants water, and fire always wants fuel. What is interesting is how both earth and fire can be seen as consuming what it receives, just as Sheol is always depicted that way. Sheol consumes the dead, and no hope is given of another kind of life.

***Eccl 9:10** Whatever your hand finds to do, do it with all your might; for there is no activity or planning or knowledge or wisdom in Sheol where you are going.*

We will re-visit Ecclesiastes chapter 9 shortly, but the point is very clear here and must be acknowledged: Sheol is a place of non-being and non-consciousness. The departed go there and cease from all activity.

Isaiah 14:9-11 *"**Sheol** from beneath is excited over you to meet you when you come; It arouses for you the spirits of the dead, all the leaders of the earth; It raises all the kings of the nations from their thrones. 10 " They will all respond and say to you, 'Even you have been made weak as we, You have become like us. 11 'Your pomp and the music of your harps have been brought down to **Sheol**; Maggots are spread out as your bed beneath you and worms are your covering."*

This prophecy is spoken against the King of Babylon, who is condemned for his oppression and arrogance. Three key points need to be observed here. First, the point of this prophecy is not to teach on the nature of Sheol, but it does serve as the context for the prophecy. Second, notice how Isaiah says that Sheol will arouse the spirits of the dead for the sake of taunting. The clear implication is that the spirits would otherwise be incapable of activity. This is in keeping with other depictions of Sheol as being a place of unconsciousness. If the deceased there were already conscious, they would not need to be aroused. Third, the reference to maggots and worms once again points to the activity of decay and destruction. Those who go to Sheol are in process of destruction and decomposition.

Hosea 13:12-14 *The iniquity of Ephraim is bound up; His sin is stored up.*

13 The pains of childbirth come upon him; He is not a wise son,
For it is not the time that he should delay at the opening of the womb.

> *14 <u>Shall I ransom them from the power of</u> **Sheol**<u>? Shall I redeem them from death</u>?*
> *O Death, where are your thorns? O **Sheol**, where is your sting? Compassion will be hidden from My sight.*

This passage is interesting for a variety of reasons, but we'll focus on the one main thought: God asks a question which expects a negative answer: will His people be ransomed from the power of Sheol, and from death? No, they will not. Within this passage, the last line, "Compassion will be hidden from My sight" clearly indicates that God will not do a heroic act to save His people in the particular time of judgment.

What is interesting about this passage is that the apostle Paul later uses it in the book of 1 Corinthians to convey the opposite point. Within Hosea, the point is that God will *not* rescue His people from death at this time. When Paul quotes Hosea, however, it is for the purpose of saying that the power of death, its sting, is removed and people will indeed be rescued from death unto life through Christ Jesus.

I have deliberately highlighted these passages above for one special reason: to give evidence that Sheol is consistently portrayed as a place of decay and unconsciousness. The ancient Hebrews generally did not look to a future existence after this life.

Having said that, the case can be driven home by the following passages, where Sheol is not always named or referred to, but the expectations clearly point in the same direction as the Sheol references above.

Genesis 3:19 *"By the sweat of your face you will eat bread, till you return to the ground,*

Because from it you were taken; For you are dust, and to dust you shall return."

This passage is famous even outside of the Bible by its use in funerals: 'Ashes to ashes, dust to dust…" This point directly parallels and reinforces what was said about Sheol throughout the previous section, that it is a place of being consumed by natural processes with no mention of an afterlife.

Job 3:13-19 *"For now I would have lain down and been quiet;*

I would have slept then, I would have been at rest,

14 With kings and with counselors of the earth, who rebuilt ruins for themselves;

15 Or with princes who had gold, who were filling their houses with silver.

16 "Or like a miscarriage which is discarded, I would not be, as infants that never saw light.

17 "There the wicked cease from raging, and there the weary are at rest.

18 "The prisoners are at ease together; they do not hear the voice of the taskmaster.

19 "The small and the great are there, and the slave is free from his master."

Everything in this section from Job screams of post-death non-existence. Job is waiting for death, for that would be preferable to him than to continue suffering as he does. If he died, he would then be like a miscarried fetus *that never had awareness*. He is a fellow mourner along with the writer of Psalm 88; living has become so painful and afterwards there is nothing to look forward to. For them, death is not a transition to a better world, just an ending to this one.

> ***Job 7:7-10*** *"Remember that my life is but breath; My eye will not again see good.*
>
> *8 "The eye of him who sees me will behold me no longer;*
>
> *Your eyes will be on me, but I will not be.*
>
> *9 "When a cloud vanishes, it is gone; so he who goes down to Sheol does not come up.*
>
> *10 "He will not return again to his house, Nor will his place know him anymore."*

The metaphor changes, but the result is the same. Just as a cloud evaporates, so does the person after death. In the future, Job says "I will not be (exist)."

> ***Psalm 30:9*** *"What profit is there in my blood, if I go down to the pit? Will the dust praise You? Will it declare Your faithfulness?"*

Like the Hosea passage earlier, the Psalmist asks a rhetorical question: once I die will I say or do anything? Once again the answer implied is "No."

> ***Ps 88:3-7, 10-12*** *For my soul has had enough troubles,*
>
> *and my life has drawn near to* ***Sheol****.*
>
> *4 I am reckoned among those who go down to the pit;*
>
> *I have become like a man without strength,*

> *5 Forsaken among the dead, like the slain who lie in the grave,*
> *Whom You remember no more, and they are cut off from Your hand.*
> *6 You have put me in the lowest pit ,in dark places, in the depths.*
> *7 Your wrath has rested upon me, and You have afflicted me with all Your waves. Selah.*
> *10 Will You perform wonders for the dead? Will the departed spirits rise and praise You?*
> *11 Will Your lovingkindness be declared in the grave, Your faithfulness in* ***Abaddon****?*
> *12 Will Your wonders be made known in the darkness?*
> *And Your righteousness in the land of forgetfulness?*

In this devastating lament by the Psalmist, the utter bleakness of life has set in. In fact, this is the only lamentation Psalm that lacks a 'pick me up.' Usually, in a lamentation Psalm, the author finds at least *something* to find comfort in; but here in Psalm 88 no comfort is found whatsoever. Having said that, let us make some observations.

First, the author is as low as he can go; "It's like I'm already dead." Life has become void of good. He has nothing left, thus he is like an occupant of Sheol. If Sheol was a place of conscious activity and motion, the comparison would not work. This lament draws upon the utter lifelessness of Sheol to make its point: "I've got absolutely no life in me anymore."

Second, the author says that the slain in the grave/ Sheol are remembered by God no more, and they are cut off from His hand. Once again, this clearly talks about all things having come to an utter end. Not even God interacts with the deceased anymore.

Third, verses 10-12 contain six rhetorical questions about what kind of future is in store for those in Sheol. Will God do anything for them, or will they praise God in any way? For all these questions, the expected answer is "No." The Psalmist laments that this life is no longer worth living, and even worse, *there is no life to come.* Like the majority of Old Testament scripture, no hope is held out for a better hereafter.

Ecclesiastes 3:19-22 *For the fate of the sons of men and the fate of beasts is the same. As one dies so dies the other; indeed, they all have the same breath and there is no advantage for man over beast, for all is vanity. 20 All go to the same place. All came from the dust and all return to the dust. 21 Who knows that the breath of man ascends upward and the breath of the beast descends downward to the earth?*

In this section of Ecclesiastes, Solomon laments very pointedly that there's no justice in death because all people die and go to the same place, regardless of virtue. There is no reward for those who lived rightly before God.

Ecclesiastes 9:4-10 *For whoever is joined with all the living, there is hope; surely a live dog is better than a dead lion. 5 For the living know they will die; but the dead do not know anything,* *nor have they any longer a reward, for their memory is forgotten. 6 <u>Indeed their love, their hate and their zeal have already perished,</u> and they will no longer have a share in all that is done under the sun. 7 Go then, eat your bread in happiness and drink your wine with a cheerful heart; for God has already approved your works. 8 Let your clothes be white all the time, and let not oil be lacking on your head. 9 Enjoy life with the woman whom you love all the days of your fleeting life which He has given to you under the sun; for this is your reward in life and in your toil in which you have labored under the sun. 10 Whatever your hand finds to do, do it with all your might; <u>for there is no activity or planning or knowledge or wisdom in Sheol where you are going.</u>*

Once again, we see Solomon level the playing field, saying there is no distinction between the righteous and the wicked after death. In this passage, he goes further, stating that the deceased have no cognitive function. Furthermore, he says that they have already perished, which the apostle Paul echoes in 1 Corinthians 15. Then finally, Solomon says in a *coup de grace,* that there is no activity, planning, knowledge or wisdom in Sheol, the point being that you'd better live well now *because there is no life to come.*

Isaiah 38:10-20 *I said, "In the middle of my life I am to enter the gates of* ***Sheol;*** *I am to be deprived of the rest of my years." 11 I said, "I will not see the LORD, The LORD in the land of the living; I will look on man no more among the inhabitants of the world. 12 "Like a shepherd's tent my dwelling is pulled up and removed from me; As a weaver I rolled up my life. <u>He cuts me off from the loom;</u> From day until night You make an end of*

me. 13 "I composed my soul until morning. Like a lion — so He
breaks all my bones, From day until night You make an end of me. 14
"Like a swallow, like a crane, so I twitter; I moan like a dove; My eyes
look wistfully to the heights; O Lord, I am oppressed, be my security.
15 " What shall I say? For He has spoken to me, and He
Himself has done it; I will wander about all my years because of
the bitterness of my soul. 16 "O Lord, by these things men live,
And in all these is the life of my spirit; O restore me to health and
let me live! 17 "Lo, for my own welfare I had great bitterness; It
is You who has kept my soul from the pit of nothingness, for You
have cast all my sins behind Your back. 18 "For Sheol cannot
thank You, Death cannot praise You; Those who go down to the
pit cannot hope for Your faithfulness. 19 "It is the living who give
thanks to You, as I do today; A father tells his sons about Your
faithfulness. 20 "The LORD will surely save me; So we will play
my songs on stringed instruments All the days of our life at the
house of the LORD."

This lamentation was composed by King Hezekiah and copied by Isaiah within his writings. Hezekiah wrote it after he was told he would die soon. Because he sought the Lord, he was granted 15 more years, and in response he wrote this psalm. The point that is driven home within his psalm is that *nothing happens after death; it's all over.* He grieves that he will no longer worship or praise God, thus underscoring once again that there was no general expectation of a future life after death for ancient Hebrews.

ABADDON

There are a few references to a place called Abaddon. This seems to be a parallelism to "Sheol" and does not contribute much to our understanding of Sheol, nor does it expand our thoughts in this area. However, in Rev. 9, we see the personification of Abaddon as the name of a death angel who leads a horde of deadly locust like creatures.

Job 26:6 "Naked is Sheol before Him, And Abaddon has no covering.

Job 28:22 "Abaddon and Death say, 'With our ears we have heard a report of it.'

Job 31:12 "For it would be fire that consumes to Abaddon, And would uproot all my increase.

Psalms 88:11 Will Your lovingkindness be declared in the grave, Your faithfulness in Abaddon?

Proverbs 15:11 Sheol and Abaddon lie open before the LORD, How much more the hearts of men!

Proverbs 27:20 Sheol and Abaddon are never satisfied, Nor are the eyes of man ever satisfied.

Revelation 9:11 They have as king over them, the angel of the abyss; his name in Hebrew is Abaddon, and in the Greek he has the name Apollyon.

SUMMARY

The weight of these passages is consistent, and they all

point in the same direction: the ancient Hebrews generally expected existence to end with death. There is no talk of immortality of the soul, there is no hope of a heaven that awaits the righteous, but rather there is the repeated lamentation that both the good and the bad go to the same place. There is no consciousness or activity in that place called Sheol.

The curse that God warned of in Genesis 3 still holds: *"in that day, you shall die."* The serpent promised immortality, but all the writers of the Old Testament testify in unison that immortality is a lie. The curse of This Age is that death reigns. Death is our enemy.

There are many other references to Sheol in the Old Testament, but they don't make my case stronger (but they don't contradict it either). Ancient Hebrews generally expected to die and go to Sheol; what they expected there is not elaborated upon, but you can see for yourself that it was not anticipated with joy or expectation of better things.

3

Hades: The New Testament Abode of the Dead

Most often, the Christian's first thoughts about the afterlife will bring up thoughts of heaven and hell. This is unfortunate, because in so doing we short circuit the complete message of scripture. There is much to straighten out in this area.

Generally speaking, the Old Testament point of view was that we die and that's it; we go to Sheol. Many people will respond by saying, "Yes, *that's the Old Testament!*" This is sloppy thinking. Both Old and New Testaments are God's revelation. If we think that in the Old Testament there is one system, and in the New Testament there is another system at work, we really complicate things. When did the switch take place? Right after Malachi? With John the Baptizer? After the resurrection? Obviously, the question is almost too ridiculous to ask. But we need an answer.

The simple truth is that *there was no such switch*, for the same system of thought found in the Hebrew scriptures is carried over into the New Testament. We have been blinded by faulty teaching, but if you let the Bible speak for itself, the consistency is startling. So let's begin by making some important clarifications.

First, there is no verse in the Bible that says that when we die we go to either heaven or hell. There isn't. There are some statements which are construed to mean that the writer was going to heaven soon. We will deal with that later.

Second, it is inaccurate and incomplete to speak merely of 'Hell.' In fact, the word 'Hell' is an English word, not a Hebrew or Greek one. So if we are going to address what the Bible says, we should use the words that the Bible uses. In the Old Testament, there are two words used in regards to the afterlife: 'Sheol' and 'Abaddon.' In the New Testament, there are three words: 'Hades', 'Gehenna', and 'Tartarus.' Hades and Tartarus are roughly equivalent, while Gehenna is substantially different, and will be dealt with in Part 3 of this book.

Third, it will be seen that there is very good reason to consider Sheol and Hades to be the same place. Neither receive much description. More importantly, the simple fact is that when the Old Testament was translated into Greek (which was done in between the Testaments, and called the Septuagint), the word they used to translate Sheol was Hades. Regardless of how the Greeks used the word Hades, the ancient Jewish translators felt Hades was the best word for the job.

Finally, when we look at the places where Hades is referred to, we will see that it falls in line with what was said about Sheol. We will see in this chapter that in regards to Biblical eschatology, they are the same place. We will also see that like Sheol, Hades is referred to but not defined or explained. The obvious reason is that the original readers probably didn't require it for it was already a familiar concept.

There are roughly a dozen references to Hades in the New Testament, and some of the uses are in parallel gospel accounts. Here they are:

Luke 10:15/Matthew 11:23 *"And you, Capernaum, will not be exalted to heaven, will you? You will be brought down to* ***Hades****!"*

Nothing is told here about Hades, but the inference is obvious: the people would rather be exalted to heaven, but they will be assigned to Hades instead. Nothing more is told to us, but the intent is to state a negative verdict, and Hades is that verdict.

Acts 2:27-29 *Because You will not abandon my soul to* ***Hades****, nor allow Your Holy One to undergo decay, You have made known to me the ways of life; You will make me full of gladness with Your presence.'*

29 "Brethren, I may confidently say to you regarding the patriarch David that he both died and was buried, and his tomb is with us to this day.

This is a New Testament quotation of Psalm 16:10

which will be covered in chapter 7. Seeing it here confirms the point made above, that the Jewish translators thought that the concept of Sheol and Hades were similar enough to use them interchangeably. In Psalm 16:10, the Hebrew phrase is "not abandon my soul to Sheol." Here the word is switched to Hades in the Greek.

Furthermore, Peter's sermon makes it clear that David is considered to still be in his grave there in Jerusalem, and they seem to actually know where it is as well. So the Old Testament says we die and rot in the grave, and Peter affirms in his sermon that this is the case. In scribing this story, Luke used the Septuagint, and thus builds the connection for us between Sheol and Hades.

This is a clear and solid demonstration that the Old and New Testament speak with one voice affirming the same truth.

> ***Matthew 16:18*** *"I also say to you that you are Peter, and upon this rock I will build My church; and the gates of* **Hades** *will not overpower it."*

Once again, we see that Hades is not described here, but it is obviously a negative connotation. Just as throughout the Old Testament "Sheol" was rendered as a destructive force of death, the same idea is present here. It may not be described, but the context makes it clear that it is not desirable.

Revelation 1:17-18 *I am the first and the last, and the living One; and I was dead, and behold, I am alive forevermore, and I have the keys of death and of Hades.*

In something that is akin to Psalm 139, Jesus attests His lordship over the underworld. His statement of having keys over death and Hades is a powerful claim to ultimate authority, and as the Resurrected One, He has the full right to make it. Just as in the Old Testament where death and Sheol are seen as a type of partnership, so are death and Hades.

Revelation 6:8 *I looked, and behold, an ashen horse; and he who sat on it had the name Death; and* ***Hades*** *was following with him. Authority was given to them over a fourth of the earth, to kill with sword and with famine and with pestilence and by the wild beasts of the earth.*

Just as in Revelation 1, the partnership of death and Hades is maintained here in chapter 6. In this case they are agents of God's wrath, let loose upon the earth in judgment upon the wicked. Recalling Jesus' claim of authority over death and Hades, here it states authority was *given to them* to do their work.

Revelation 20:12-14 *And I saw the dead, the great and the small, standing before the throne, and books were opened; and another book was opened, which is the book of life; and the dead were judged from the things which were written in the books, according to their deeds. 13 And the sea gave up the dead which were in it, and*

Death and Hades gave up the dead which were in them; and they were judged, every one of them according to their deeds.

This is a very powerful passage and crucial to our understanding of the unity of scripture. The scene is judgment day (which will be covered in Part 2 of this book), and the books are open to render God's verdict. The parallels and connections to the Old Testament view of Sheol are entirely consistent with this passage.

The most important point to make regarding this passage is that those being judged are being delivered up from the *deceased* state. In fact, in referring to them, John does not use the word 'revived' or 'resurrected;' he uses the word 'dead.' This is not accidental. In the Garden, God said, "You will die." Here, *the dead* are brought forth for judgment.

Furthermore, notice that the sea and death and Hades all give up the dead for judgment. The Old Testament said all people go to Sheol. Peter said in Acts 2 that David was dead and rotting in his grave. Peter also says that Jesus, and *only* Jesus has escaped from Hades. Everyone else is in this crowd waiting for judgment.

To reiterate the point made in the introduction of this book, if we die and go to heaven or hell, then this passage becomes redundant or anachronistic or flat out misleading. The dead must be brought up for judgment. Furthermore, none of the 'defendants' in Revelation 20 are said to be 'brought down from heaven' for this judgment. Again, that would be completely backwards; if they were in heaven, the point of the verdict would be moot, as they would already have received their reward.

So what we see here is a clear re-affirming of the Old Testament witness: all people die and go to Sheol/Hades, and it is from there that they await judgment.

TARTARUS

2 Peter 2:4 For if God did not spare angels when they sinned, but cast them into ***hell*** *and committed them to pits of darkness, reserved for judgment…*

The Greek word for hell here is Tartarus, and this is the only time it is used in Scripture; therefore, it does not tell us much for our study.

The Special and Difficult Case: Luke 16:19-31

I'd like to be able to say that my argument is iron clad and airtight, but it isn't. The single most difficult challenge to this is found in Luke 16, where Jesus tells a parable about Lazarus and the Rich Man:

Luke 16:19-31 *"Now there was a rich man, and he habitually dressed in purple and fine linen, joyously living in splendor every day. 20 "And a poor man named Lazarus was laid at his gate, covered with sores, 21 and longing to be fed with the crumbs which were falling from the rich man's table; besides, even the dogs were coming and licking his sores. 22 "Now the poor man died and was carried away by the angels to Abraham's bosom; and the rich man also died and was buried. 23 "In Hades he lifted up his eyes, being* *in torment, and saw Abraham far away and Lazarus in his bosom. 24 "And he cried out and said, 'Father Abraham, have mercy on me, and send Lazarus so that he may dip the tip of his finger in water and cool off my tongue, for I am in agony in this flame.' 25 "But Abraham said, 'Child, remember that during your life you received your good things, and likewise Lazarus bad things; but now he is being comforted here, and you are in agony. 26 'And besides all this, between us and you there is a great chasm fixed, so that those who wish to come over from here to you will not be able, and that none may cross over from there to us.' 27 "And he said, 'Then I beg you, father, that you send him to my father's house — 28 for I have five brothers — in order that he may warn them, so that they will not also come to this place of torment.' 29 "But Abraham said, 'They have Moses and the Prophets; let them hear them.' 30 "But he said, 'No, father Abraham, but if someone goes to them from the dead, they will repent!' 31 "But he said to him, 'If they do not listen to Moses and the Prophets, they will not be persuaded even if someone rises from the dead.'"*

There's no way around the difficulties presented in this parable. There are several problems that it presents to the otherwise consistent Biblical viewpoint as I present it. First, it implies that there is consciousness after death, regardless of righteousness or wickedness; this contradicts the Old Testament angle which has already been presented. Second, it implies that the judgment is immediate upon death. This book makes the case later that judgment, among other things, is anchored in the

Day of Yahweh. Revelation 20 supports this view, as well. *But Luke 16 presents another scenario.* Third, it clearly refers to Hades as being a place of torment. This contradicts the Old Testament view of Sheol and the other New Testament accounts of Hades.

The point of this parable is not to teach about the afterlife. Jesus previously had been teaching that it is easier for heaven and earth to pass away than for one letter or stroke of the law to fail. The end of the parable states that the rich man's relatives have the law of Moses to guide them and that a supernatural visit would not change anything. The primary problem is an attitude of disobedience. *THAT* is the point of the parable.

Some have pointed out that it nowhere says that this story *is* a parable, but I think it clearly is. But that doesn't negate the fact that Jesus presents an eschatology that is inconsistent with the rest of Scripture. A parable only works if it is consistent with how symbols are understood. It has to have parallels with the perceived operations of the listener's world. That's why the parable of the Good Samaritan is powerful. The Samaritans were despised in proper Israel, and by making him the hero of the story, Jesus is saying that your neighbor may be someone you are normally prejudiced against.

If this were a contested part of the ancient Greek manuscripts, we might argue that it is a spurious addition added later, but that case cannot be made. This story is in the earliest manuscripts we have. We can't just eject it with good cause.

So the reality is this: *I cannot refute the implications of this parable, and the fact that it is a parable doesn't let me off the hook;* having said that, I can truthfully say that it is the only legitimate challenge to the presentation offered in this book. Other objections will be addressed later; but here, I can only admit that I don't have a good answer.

SUMMARY

The Old Testament repeatedly and consistently states that people die and go to the place called Sheol, a place of non-existence. Later, we will talk about how the Old Testament hints about a future reward and resurrection, but for now we will leave it at this.

The New Testament says a similar thing, that people die and rest in non-existence, and more will be said in the following chapter on this. Ancient Jews used the word 'Hades' to translate the Hebrew word 'Sheol' and we see the New Testament writers use this word to refer to the destination of the deceased. *The Old and New Testament are in agreement on this.* Later, we will see that the New Testament adds the promise of another life to come, but that is not contained within the concept of Hades. We will see later that the life to come is received *after* Hades.

This may sound tenuous and questionable, so we will proceed to the next chapter and consider the phrase "asleep in Christ" and see that its usage reinforces the ideas laid out already.

4

Asleep In Christ

The phrase "asleep in Christ" occurs repeatedly in the New Testament. Because we've gotten our traditional theology all patched together from different ideas rather than taking scripture as a whole, this concept gets ignored far too often. In fact, if you bring it up in conversation, most Christians will have a frightened look in their eyes as though you've conjured up some wild idea.

If you study about Sheol in the Old Testament and then add to that the New Testament depiction of Hades, then 'asleep in Christ' fits right in and proves to be very consistent with the previous findings.

Before we get underway in studying this, I want to make a noteworthy point: in the Old Testament, the phrase "and slept with his fathers" occurs 36 times. In each case it refers to someone who died. As we saw earlier, in his sermon at Pentecost, Peter referred to King

David as dead and still buried in Jerusalem. In 1 Kings 2:10, 'slept with his fathers' is used in reference to him, and a thousand years later, he is still seen as simply dead. Having said that, let us begin our study of this phrase, "Asleep in Christ."

> ***Matthew 9:24-26*** *He said, "Leave; for the girl has not died, but is asleep." And they began laughing at Him. 25 But when the crowd had been sent out, He entered and took her by the hand, and the girl got up. 26 This news spread throughout all that land.*

It is obvious from this passage that the little girl is dead, and that Jesus is being metaphorical when He says she is asleep. He knows He will raise her from the dead, so from His perspective she *is* merely sleeping. The mockery of Jesus on this point is that He obviously is a fool to think she's not dead. The use of the sleeping metaphor by Jesus is entirely in keeping with the rest of the New Testament.

> ***John 11:12-15*** *The disciples then said to Him, "Lord, if he has fallen asleep, then he will recover." 13 Now Jesus had spoken of his death, but they thought that He was speaking of literal sleep. 14 So Jesus then said to them plainly, "Lazarus is dead,*

In this story, Jesus and the disciples are on the way to see Lazarus, who is seriously ill. Jesus deliberately stalls, knowing that Lazarus will die. Once again, Jesus says 'sleep' when He clearly means dead, and in this story we get the added benefit of Jesus making plain what was implied in the last story: He uses 'sleep' as a metaphor for death.

Acts 7:58-60 *They went on stoning Stephen as he called on the Lord and said, "Lord Jesus, receive my spirit!" 60 Then falling on his knees, he cried out with a loud voice, "Lord, do not hold this sin against them!" Having said this,* ***he fell asleep****.*

From the story, it is plain to see that Stephen has been stoned to death; this was an execution. The perspective is given from a Christian point of view, that death for the believer is only a pause before the resurrection. Everyone reading this story knows that Stephen is dead.

Acts 13:36-38 *"For David, after he had served the purpose of God in his own generation,* ***fell asleep****, and was laid among his fathers and underwent decay; 37 but He whom God raised did not undergo decay.*

Once again King David is used as an example of someone truly dead. A key element is that the Apostle Paul is referencing Psalm 16, which states that God will not allow His Holy One to undergo decay. Just as Peter did before him, Paul states this to show that the Psalm was written about the Messiah Jesus, not King David. David *did* die and undergo decay, *but Jesus didn't.* And like Peter, Paul emphasizes that David is dead, "asleep." The key point here is that "asleep" is clearly a reference to having passed away.

1 Corinthians 15:5-8 *After that He appeared to more than five hundred brethren at one time, most of whom remain until now, but some have fallen asleep; 7 then He appeared to James, then to all the apostles; 8 and last of all, as to one untimely born, He appeared to me also.*

Here, Paul is referring to the fact that the resurrected

Jesus had appeared to many witnesses, even five hundred at one time. He says most are still alive, but some have "fallen asleep," or in other words, died.

> ***1 Corinthians 15:16-19*** *For if the dead are not raised, not even Christ has been raised; 17 and if Christ has not been raised, your faith is worthless; you are still in your sins. 18 Then those also who have fallen asleep have perished.*

This passage is vitally important to our study. Paul is arguing three points. First, there *is* a general resurrection; second, that Jesus *was* resurrected; and three, that if Jesus wasn't resurrected, then the Christian faith is null and void. But notice this very important point: if Jesus wasn't resurrected, *then the deceased have already perished.*

Ask yourself a very important question: if people die and go to heaven, how could they still be in danger of perishing? Paul is saying that the only hope the deceased have is that Jesus will resurrect them in the future, but if there is no resurrection, then *they are already gone.* Paul couldn't say this if he believed people died and go to heaven; the deceased believers would be considered safe and secure in heaven, and in no danger. Instead, Paul believes that they, like King David, are in the ground and decomposing, and if there is no resurrection, then they are gone for good.

> ***1 Thessalonians 4:13-16*** *But we do not want you to be uninformed, brethren, about those who are asleep, so that you will not grieve as do the rest who have no hope. 14 For if we believe that Jesus died and rose again, even so God will bring with Him those*

<u>who have fallen asleep in Jesus</u>. For this we say to you by the word of the Lord, that we who are alive and remain until the coming of the Lord, will not precede <u>those who have fallen asleep</u>. 16 For the Lord Himself will descend from heaven with a shout, with the voice of the archangel and with the trumpet of God, and <u>the dead in Christ will rise first</u>.

This passage has two main subject matters: the return of Christ, and the resurrection of His saints. The believers in Thessalonica apparently were worried about those who had died. Would they miss out on the glory which comes with the return of Christ? Paul says no. He wants them to have hope, and the hope he gives them is that those who have fallen asleep will be resurrected by Christ to meet with those who are still alive.

The phrasing is awkward, as it sounds as though Jesus would be bringing those asleep in Christ with Him from somewhere else. Consequently, some jump to the conclusion that this means He is bringing them from heaven. But as we have seen in the previous passage, Paul does *not* say that the deceased believers are in heaven; they are dead and waiting the resurrection at the hand of Jesus. And, if the dead will be raised first, from whence are they being raised? If they are 'in heaven' with Him, then 'being raised' would be a strange way to put it. More on this later.

1 Thessalonians 5:9-10 *For God has not destined us for wrath, but for obtaining salvation through our Lord Jesus Christ, who died for us, so that <u>whether we are awake or asleep</u>, we will live together with Him.*

This passage will figure in future arguments later, but for now the key point is that Paul refers to 'awake or asleep'. It is clear that he means 'dead or alive.' Again, his comfort is that nobody gets lost to Christ; He will keep them all and all will live with Him in the resurrection.

2 Peter 3:3-5 *Know this first of all, that in the last days mockers will come with their mocking, following after their own lusts, 4 and saying, "Where is the promise of His coming? For ever since the fathers fell asleep, all continues as it was from the beginning of creation."*

This verse simply underscores again that 'asleep' was a Christian idiom for referring to death.

TRICKY PASSAGES:

As I did in the last chapter, I want to include problematic passages. It can be said that the following verses do not raise as much challenge as Luke 16 did, but they should still be addressed.

Luke 23:43 *And He said to him, "Truly I say to you, today you shall be with Me in Paradise."*

As I discuss the teaching contained in this study, this is the verse that comes up the most. The brigand is dying on the cross alongside Jesus, and is repentant and remorseful. He recognizes something in Jesus and knows that he needs to reconcile to it. Jesus promises him that they will be together in paradise.

To begin with, although we often infer it, Jesus did *not* say "you will die and go to heaven today." He said, "You will be with Me in paradise." They are not the same thing. Recognize the situation. They are both dying in excruciating pain; there's no time to lose, and time is of the essence. What is Jesus' prime objective? It is to bring quick assurance and comfort to a repentant sinner. There's no time for a long explanation of theology and salvation. There's no time for a discussion as to what the man knows and believes. So with almost no time to work with, Jesus comforts the man and says "You will be with Me." That's all the man desires. Did he know that Jesus' death would bring salvation to the world? Did he know Jesus was the Messiah? Was he a practicing Jew? None of this is known, and it doesn't matter. In a quick emergency operation, Jesus simply wants to give a quick word to ease the man's mind. We shouldn't read too much into it.

> ***2 Corinthians 5:6-8*** *Therefore, being always of good courage, and knowing that while we are at home in the body we are absent from the Lord — 7 for we walk by faith, not by sight — 8 we are of good courage, I say, and prefer rather to be absent from the body and to be at home with the Lord.*

Here Paul seems to speaking in terms of Greek thought, "in the body," "absent from the body" and so on. To 'be at home with the Lord' at first glance would seem to mean "go to heaven" but again, this is reading theology *into* the text. Like the brigand on the cross, the comfort is that after death, we will be in the care of the Lord, and that will be much more peaceful than life in the suffering world.

Philippians 1:22-25 *But I am hard-pressed from both directions, having the desire to depart and be with Christ, for that is very much better; 24 yet to remain on in the flesh is more necessary for your sake.*

"Depart and be with Christ" like the previous passage above, again sounds to us to mean "Die and go to heaven," and again that is reading *into* the text. Paul is not picturing his soul leaving his body to go to heaven; he is trusting Jesus to watch over him after death until the resurrection, just as our citizenship is being preserved for us in heaven from whence it will come to us in the future.

In these three passages, we see a parallel to a Jewish idiom. Jews often referred to being in the 'bosom of Abraham.' In fact, this phrase is used in Luke 16, and was a common expression. It was not defined or spelled out, but the thought was that by virtue of being a child of Abraham, Jews would be nestled into his watchful care. Again, no theology was worked out for this, nor was it explained in scripture. The important point is that "To be with Jesus" was a re-working of the phrase "In the bosom of Abraham." It is not meant as a precise theological teaching but as a quick reassuring phrase for God's people.

SUMMARY

The idea that "asleep in Christ" refers to the deceased is not difficult to fathom. Even the beginning novice in Bible study can readily see that this sleep language is a metaphor. What is more challenging is to see all the ramifications.

First, if we die and go to heaven, 'asleep' is really a backwards way to describe the heavenly afterlife. If people are running around in heaven in a state of bliss, how could that in any way be considered a form of 'sleep'? No, something else is at work here. Just as Sheol is a place of non-being, and Hades is the Greek equivalent, then it makes more sense that those who are 'asleep in Christ' are in those places of non-being and non-consciousness.

Second, Paul's argument in 1 Corinthians is crucial: he says those who are asleep in Christ have already perished if there is no resurrection. If he believed people die and go to heaven, then his argument wouldn't make sense; those who have died and gone to heaven have made it safely home and have nothing to worry about.

Third, an idea we have not yet considered is one I hear frequently: that 'asleep in Christ' refers to just the body, not the soul. There are three major problems with this approach. A) The Jews did not partition out body, soul and spirit in their world view. They took a holistic approach that the person is one unified being. Some of the Greeks believed in compartmentalizing human beings into material and non-material parts. B) Some say that the rising of the dead is the re-uniting of the body and soul, *but the Bible nowhere says that body and soul are separated and then rejoined.* This is a manufactured answer that becomes required when the unity of Scripture is ignored. Paul *never* says that those who are asleep in Christ will be reunited with their souls. C) Again, when he says the resurrection is the only hope of the deceased (and he clearly states this), was this hope only for their bodies? He *didn't* say that if there is no resurrection, then the *bodies* of the deceased are already perished; the very clear implication is that the whole person is gone, not just part of them.

Fourth, the New Testament drew upon the stories of Old Testament saints and *not once* was it said that the ancient fathers died and went to a better place. Quite the opposite: as we saw, at least twice David was clearly said to be dead and decomposing with no hint of him being in heaven or such thing. Rather, David was the chief contrast with the living Christ, on Whom all the deceased are counting upon for a future life.

Just as the Old Testament shows Sheol as the place of the unconscious dead, and the New Testament used 'Hades' to refer to this same place, now the term 'asleep in Christ' maintains the same thought: the deceased are really dead, and awaiting the coming of Jesus in glory for their resurrection.

Part 1 Summary

We've gotten started in our study, and laid the foundation. If you were raised in a traditional Christian home, some of these ideas might have come at you from left field and caught you off guard. Yet, the points made have also been shown to be very Biblical. It will serve us well to consider what these main points are.

First, in chapter one, it was established that the fall of humanity in the Garden of Eden was where we lost the chance for immortality. The serpent lied and said we would not die, and believing that, Adam & Eve ate of the tree of knowledge of good & evil. This point is underscored by the actions of God shortly thereafter: the way to the tree of life was cut off precisely *to prevent immortality.*

If people want to believe in an immortal soul, that's their freedom; but it cannot be said to be a Biblical teaching. Genesis 3 eliminates that option, and there is no verse anywhere in scripture that says the soul *is* immortal.

This point is important for three reasons: A) When we discuss the eternal future, we cannot begin with the assumption that we inherently have life within us. The goal of humanity is to secure life for ourselves, and for it to be worth living. When discussing the future of our existence, we need to realize that the future is already lost and must be regained. B) When we assume that the soul is immortal, then the next leap is to say that upon death, the soul must go somewhere. But if you don't assume immortality, then a different question arises: *How will we get life back again?* When Jesus says that He came "to give us life, and that, abundantly" some say that He means a good eternal life over a nasty eternal life. This is because they assume the immortality of the soul. But if we do not inherently have immortality, then it becomes much more stark and literal: Jesus is saying He will give us life *where we would have none at all, period!* C) For our own personal piety, we need to be humble before our Creator and realize that in order to live, *HE* must give us life. It is the hubris of humanity to think we will live forever regardless of what God says or thinks. No, according to the whole of scripture, we will only have life if He bequeaths it to us.

Second, we saw that throughout the Old Testament, there was generally no expectation for an afterlife. Sheol is the name of the place to which the departed go, and although it is never described fully, it is clear from the tone of the relevant passages that nothing happens there.

Anyone who reads the Old Testament in comparison to the New can clearly see that there is a bleakness that the Christian message overcomes. There was no talk of departing for another, better world, but instead, a grieving for the end of life. Repeatedly, the phrase "Slept with his fathers" is used of the deceased, and nothing is said to ease the pain.

Recently, some writers have said that the description of Sheol is that it is a place of conscious existence, but this is clearly false and untrue. The reason that the lamenting Psalms are so potent is that they were grieving deeply over the end of life. Sheol was absolutely not another name for heaven, nor was anything positive said about it. The entire stance of the Old Testament views the human condition as completely mortal through and through. Greeks believed in an immortal soul, but very clearly, the Hebrews did not.

Third, we showed that Hades was the New Testament equivalent of Sheol. In fact, when the Jews translated the Old Testament into Greek, the word they used for 'Sheol' was 'Hades.' Contrary to popular thought, the New Testament writers did not switch gears and begin teaching an immortal soul or about dying and going to heaven. They *retained* the Old Testament perspective of mortality.

Hades is seen as the destination of people after death, and apart from Luke 16, nothing is said about a conscious existence. Just as it happens with Sheol, Hades is said to be the destination of the deceased, but then is not described in any detail.

Most importantly, 'Hell' is a very inaccurate and misleading word to toss around. There are three New Testament place names for after death: Hades, Tarturus and Gehenna (to be discussed in a later chapter). Gehenna is very different from Hades *and they are not interchangeable.*

Fourth, consistent with all the above is the New Testament phrase, "Asleep in Christ." When seen in context of all the above, the idiom makes perfect sense. If people die and go to Sheol/Hades, and if this 'place' is unconscious non-existence as the Old Testament describes, *then 'sleeping' in Christ is the perfect match to this theology.* If we die and go to heaven (or hell), then the phrase 'sleeping in Christ' is a great mismatch. Yet this is the term which is repeatedly and clearly used of deceased believers. As we said, this New Testament phrase continues the line of "… and slept with his fathers" which was used in the Old Testament, and parallels the Hebrew idiom "In the bosom of Abraham."

If the deceased believers die and go to heaven, then 'asleep' is hardly the word to use to describe the situation. People try to resolve this dilemma by saying that 'asleep' refers to the body, and that the soul is separated at death and goes elsewhere. *The Bible nowhere says this!* Nor does it say that at some point down the road, the soul and body are reunited. This is a solution that is forced into our theology when we ignore the whole of scripture. It also is rooted in the belief in an immortal soul, which I have shown to be a false idea. Because people start with the wrong presupposition, they have to resort to weak patch jobs to keep their theology together.

This Age is the era of death and mortality. The lie of the serpent in the Garden of Eden was "You will not die!" This was a false promise of immortality, and in the name of Christian theology, this lie has continued to be propagated. When Jesus promised eternal life, it was with the Jewish understanding that there otherwise will be no life at all.

Part Two: The Day of the Lord

In this section, we see how the Old Testament concept of the Day of Yahweh was retained and refitted as a Christian doctrine. Originally an idea to give comfort to God's people, it also became a threat of judgment over Israel herself, and not just the nations.

Paul takes the idea of this awesome day and wraps it around the Messiah: Jesus of Nazareth. This is a profound statement about who Jesus is, but also is clearly tied to the Christian promise of His return and our resurrection from the dead.

5. The Day of YHWH (Old Testament)
6. The Day of Jesus Christ (New Testament)
7. The Return of Jesus
8. The Resurrection

5

The Day of Yahweh (Old Testament)

Although not referred to in the earlier parts of the Old Testament, the Day of Yahweh (henceforth called DOY) becomes a dominant feature in the Prophets and casts a shadow over everything. Many times it is called by its full name, but other times it is hinted at by the phrase "On that day" or "In that day." Jesus and Paul will be seen to use this term as well, again showing that the New Testament retains the Jewish framework of the Old.

Because this vital concept has been overlooked and neglected by many Christian theologians, eschatology has become unbiblical and unnecessarily complicated. The DOY is the great hinge point in between This Age and The Age to Come. The promises and hopes that lie within The Age to Come are fulfilled because of the DOY, so it is important to have a firm understanding of it.

We will find that this idea is multi-faceted, flexible and transformational.

> ***Isaiah 13:6-12:*** *Wail, for the* ***day of the LORD*** *is near!*
>
> *It will come as* destruction *from the Almighty.*
>
> *7 Therefore all hands will fall limp, and every man's heart will melt.*
>
> *8 They will be terrified, pains and anguish will take hold of them;*
>
> *They will writhe like a woman in labor,*
>
> *They will look at one another in astonishment, their faces aflame.*
>
> *9 Behold,* ***the day of the LORD*** *is coming, cruel, with fury and burning anger,*
>
> *To make the land a desolation; And He will exterminate its sinners from it.*
>
> *10 For the stars of heaven and their constellations will not flash forth their light;*
>
> *The sun will be dark when it rises*
>
> *11 Thus I will punish the world for its evil and the wicked for their iniquity;*
>
> *I will also put an end to the arrogance of the proud and abase the haughtiness of the ruthless.*
>
> *12 I will make mortal man scarcer than pure gold and mankind than the gold of Ophir.*

In what is possibly the earliest mention of the DOY, the context is a prophecy against Babylon. In the immediate sense, God is rebuking Babylon for its wars and destruction. God warns of great pain and anguish that He will bring to them, with the result that the sinners will be exterminated from the land (vs. 9).

However, there is a strong indication of a wider application. In vs. 11, God says He will punish *the world* for its evil, and this seems to point to a judgment beyond the immediate situation regarding Babylon. In vs. 12, notice the reference to mortal man, and the prediction of his scarcity.

> ***Joel 1:15-20*** *15 Alas for the day! For the* ***day of the LORD*** *is near, and it will come as destruction from the Almighty.*
>
> *16 Has not food been cut off before our eyes, gladness and joy from the house of our God?*
>
> *17 The seeds shrivel under their clods; The storehouses are desolate, the barns are torn down, for the grain is dried up.*
>
> *18 How the beasts groan! The herds of cattle wander aimlessly*
>
> *Because there is no pasture for them; even the flocks of sheep suffer.*
>
> *19 To You, O LORD, I cry; for fire has devoured the pastures of the wilderness And the flame has burned up all the trees of the field.*
>
> *20 Even the beasts of the field pant for You; For the water brooks are dried up And fire has devoured the pastures of the wilderness.*

The Minor Prophet Joel has the DOY as his central theme, so every chapter is a warning about it. The message has the immediate focus upon a locust invasion, which in this case would be far more severe than usual. It is clearly meant to point to events happening soon after the message. Within this one passage there nothing to point beyond the imminent destruction that will befall Israel, but the thoroughly destructive nature of the DOY is of interest to us.

> ***Joel 2:1-3*** *Blow a trumpet in Zion, And sound an alarm on My holy mountain!*
>
> *Let all the inhabitants of the land tremble, For the day of the LORD is coming; Surely it is near,*
>
> *2 A day of darkness and gloom, A day of clouds and thick darkness.*
>
> *As the dawn is spread over the mountains, So there is a great and mighty people;*
>
> *There has never been anything like it, Nor will there be again after it*
>
> *To the years of many generations.*
>
> *3 A fire consumes before them And behind them a flame burns.*
>
> *The land is like the garden of Eden before them But a desolate wilderness behind them,*
>
> *And nothing at all escapes them.*

Once again, as it is in the previous passage, this prophecy is about an imminent locust invasion, that is reckoned as the DOY. Again, it is thoroughly destructive.

Joel 2:11 *The LORD utters His voice before His army; Surely His camp is very great. For strong is he who carries out His word.* ***The Day of the LORD*** *is indeed great and very awesome, and who can endure it?*

Again, the context is the coming locust invasion.

Joel 2:30-32 *"I will display wonders in the sky and on the earth; blood, fire and columns of smoke.*
The sun will be turned into darkness and the moon into blood before the great and awesome **day of the Lord** *comes.*
And it will come about that whoever calls upon the name of the Lord will be delivered;
For on Mount Zion and in Jerusalem, there will be those who will escape,
As the Lord has said, even among the survivors whom the Lord calls.

This is where the plot thickens. We join the passage actually at midpoint, following the prediction that in the last days there will be visions and spiritual manifestations. What is of particular interest to us is that at this point, the DOY takes on a wider meaning, and obviously there has been a shift in emphasis. The focus is not upon the locust invasion here but upon cataclysmic events down the road. This is apocalyptic language, foreboding, mysterious and dark. The DOY is taking on characteristics far more frightening than a locust invasion.

But there is a sound of hope that previous references lacked: the DOY is a day of deliverance for God's people.

We will see this aspect expanded upon in Paul's writings. The DOY is destruction and deliverance both, which is a very Old Testament styled motif.

What is also noteworthy about this passage is that this is what Peter quotes on Pentecost Sunday when preaching to the various peoples. His declaration there is that what they are witnessing is *a* day of the Lord; however, what we will see later, from the apostle Paul is his ironclad insistence that the DOY has *not* happened yet. Why is this?

What we have seen already in Joel provides an answer: the DOY is something that happens both *within* history, and *to end it.* Joel said the locust invasion of his day was a Day of the Lord, but he clearly is pointing to something else entirely later on and calling *that* THE day of the Lord as well. This shows us how flexible the term is. Events of God's judgment within This Age can be called the Day of the Lord, but the *ultimate, true* DOY is the final day of both deliverance and destruction.

Joel 3:11-17 *Hasten and come, all you surrounding nations, And gather yourselves there. Bring down, O LORD, Your mighty ones. 12 Let the nations be aroused And come up to the valley of Jehoshaphat, For there I will sit to judge All the surrounding nations.*

13 Put in the sickle, for the harvest is ripe. Come, tread, for the wine press is full; The vats overflow, for their wickedness is great. 14 Multitudes, multitudes in the valley of decision! For the ***day of the LORD*** *is near in the valley of decision.*

15 The sun and moon grow dark and the stars lose their brightness.

16 The LORD roars from Zion and utters His voice from Jerusalem, and the heavens and the earth tremble. But the LORD is a refuge for His people and a stronghold to the sons of Israel.

17 Then you will know that I am the LORD your God dwelling in Zion, My holy mountain. So Jerusalem will be holy, and strangers will pass through it no more.

This passage reiterates points made previously. There is a universal scope to the DOY here. Apocalyptic language points to a massive event. The DOY is seen as both horribly destructive and a day of deliverance for God's people, who will be spared the wrath being inflicted everywhere.

Amos 5:18-20 *Alas, you who are longing for the* ***day of the LORD,***

For what purpose will the ***day of the LORD*** *be to you?*

It will be darkness and not light;

19 As when a man flees from a lion and a bear meets him,

Or goes home, leans his hand against the wall and a snake bites him.

20 Will not the day of the LORD be darkness instead of light,

Even gloom with no brightness in it?

This is a parody by Amos toward a misguided hope. Israel was in a time of great economic oppression against the poor while clinging to nationalistic pride. Amos arrived to say that their hope in Yahweh was misplaced while they rode on the backs of the poor. So he takes an idea which has taken root in their collective consciousness - the DOY – and tells them that it will backfire against them. They see themselves as waiting for His deliverance, and instead, God says it will be a day of destruction for them.

> ***Ezekiel 30:1-4*** *The word of the LORD came again to me saying,*
>
> *2 "Son of man, prophesy and say, 'Thus says the Lord GOD, "Wail, 'Alas for the day!'*
>
> *3 "For the day is near, even* ***the day of the LORD*** *is near;*
>
> *It will be a day of clouds, a time of doom for the nations.*
>
> *4 "A sword will come upon Egypt, and anguish will be in Ethiopia; When the slain fall in Egypt, they take away her wealth, and her foundations are torn down.*

This is a case of where the DOY is clearly within history, rather than an apocalyptic setting. It is a prophecy against Egypt and her allies, given because of their conspiracy against Israel.

> ***Obadiah 15-18*** *"For the* ***day of the LORD*** *draws near on all the nations.*
>
> *As you have done, it will be done to you. Your dealings will return on your own head.*
>
> *16 "Because just as you drank on My holy mountain, all the nations will drink continually.*
>
> *They will drink and swallow and become as if they had never existed.*
>
> *17 "But on Mount Zion there will be those who escape, and it will be holy.*
>
> *And the house of Jacob will possess their possessions.*

18 "Then the house of Jacob will be a fire and the house of Joseph a flame;

But the house of Esau will be as stubble. And they will set them on fire and consume them, so that there will be no survivor of the house of Esau," for the LORD has spoken.

Here, the application seems to be immediate while serving as a warning for the ultimate future as well. The entire book of Obadiah is a prophecy against Edom, the descendants of Esau for their corrupt dealings with Israel. The exact historical setting is uncertain, but the tone of this passage hints at something on a wider scale than just Edom's immediate future. Once again, the DOY is a double edged sword; it is destruction for God's enemies, but deliverance for His people.

Zephaniah 1 *The word of the LORD which came to Zephaniah son of Cushi, son of Gedaliah, son of Amariah, son of Hezekiah, in the days of Josiah son of Amon, king of Judah:*

2 "I will completely remove all things from the face of the earth," declares the LORD.

3 "I will remove man and beast; I will remove the birds of the sky and the fish of the sea, And the ruins along with the wicked; And I will cut off man from the face of the earth," declares the LORD.

4 "So I will stretch out My hand against Judah and against all the inhabitants of Jerusalem. And I will cut off the remnant of Baal from this place, and the names of the idolatrous priests along with the priests.

5 "And those who bow down on the housetops to the host of heaven, and those who bow down and swear to the LORD and yet swear by Milcom, 6 and those who have turned back from following the LORD, and those who have not sought the LORD or inquired of Him."

7 Be silent before the Lord GOD! For the ***day of the LORD*** *is near, for the LORD has prepared a sacrifice, He has consecrated His guests.*

8 "Then it will come about on the day of the LORD'S sacrifice that I will punish the princes, the king's sons and all who clothe themselves with foreign garments.

9 "And I will punish on that day all who leap on the temple threshold, who fill the house of their lord with violence and deceit.

10 "On that day," declares the LORD, "There will be the sound of a cry from the Fish Gate, A wail from the Second Quarter, and a loud crash from the hills.

11 "Wail, O inhabitants of the Mortar, for all the people of Canaan will be silenced; All who weigh out silver will be cut off.

12 "It will come about at that time that I will search Jerusalem with lamps, And I will punish the men who are stagnant in spirit, who say in their hearts, 'The LORD will not do good or evil!'

13 "Moreover, their wealth will become plunder and their houses desolate; Yes, they will build houses but not inhabit them, and plant vineyards but not drink their wine."

14 Near is ***the great day of the LORD****, near and coming very quickly; Listen,* ***the day of the LORD****! In it the warrior cries out bitterly.*

15 A day of wrath is that day, A day of trouble and distress, A day of destruction and desolation, A day of darkness and gloom, A day of clouds and thick darkness,

16 A day of trumpet and battle cry against the fortified cities and the high corner towers.

17 I will bring distress on men so that they will walk like the blind, because they have sinned against the LORD; And their blood will be poured out like dust and their flesh like dung.

18 Neither their silver nor their gold will be able to deliver them On the day of the LORD'S wrath; And all the earth will be devoured In the fire of His jealousy, for He will make a complete end, indeed a terrifying one, of all the inhabitants of the earth.

In what is perhaps the most sobering and frightening depiction, Zephaniah leaves little room for doubt about the severity of the DOY. While it is reasonable to ask how much of the wording is hyperbole, there is also a clear indication of larger themes. The overwhelming tone is one of utter destruction. Two other features bear closer scrutiny. First, is the phrase, "On that day" in vs. 10. This phrase is seen repeatedly in the Old Testament, and often points to themes seen in the DOY without using that term specifically. Second, one can see the influence of this language upon the Apostle Paul's writings. He too uses the idea of wrath in his language, and as we will see in the next chapter, his idea of the DOY seems to fit right within this kind of outlook.

Malachi 4:5-6 *"Behold, I am going to send you Elijah the prophet before the coming of the great and terrible* ***day of the LORD****. 6 "He will restore the hearts of the fathers to their children and the hearts of the children to their fathers, so that I will not come and smite the land with a curse."*

This famous passage is referred to by Jesus as having already been fulfilled in John the Baptizer. The implication seems to be that since the return of Elijah has been fulfilled, then Jesus' ministry can be considered to be a type of DOY. As we'll see again later, this shows that there is some flexibility regarding the DOY in how it's used.

SUMMARY

If one does a survey of all the times "In that day" or "On that day" is used and take note of the tone, it is clear that many times it sounds very similar to the concept of the DOY. Like the DOY, the term can be both an imminent event or a far off, ultimate judgment. Because there are so many instances (over one hundred), I've chosen to not include all of them in this study. But the reader will notice this thread throughout their reading of both the Old and New Testaments. Having said that, let's review the points we've covered in this chapter.

First, the DOY is a term which describes brutal judgment and punishment. There is often a tone of finality to its use that is inescapable. There is no escaping the sense of harsh justice which God speaks in these moments.

Second, the DOY is often used to describe both God's judgment *within* history, and *to end it.* Israel faced several "Days of the LORD." Joel provides a quick example, where he describes a severe locust invasion as being the DOY. Yet there are other times when the cataclysmic language points to something far more devastating. When Zephaniah quotes Yahweh as saying He will remove all inhabitants from the earth, it is difficult to turn that into a metaphor. One difficulty: it says that God will remove "all things"; however, based upon all other references, it is safe to say that it likely means all *unrighteous* things.

Third, we see that the DOY sometimes also includes an element of deliverance which is promised to the faithful. We will see this echoed in Paul's writings in the next chapter. If we keep all these ideas close at hand, we will see that the DOY was not a bogeyman set within the Old Testament for Israel, and then forgotten, but instead is deeply enmeshed into the New Testament theology as well, and is not only retained, but amplified and incorporated into the person of Jesus Christ.

6

The Day of Jesus Christ (New Testament)

In chapter 5, we surveyed the term and ideas of the Day Of Yahweh. In this chapter, we will see how this concept did not pass away with the Old Testament, but actually was an integral part of the theology of Jesus and Paul. The threats and promises of the DOY are still in effect, and still a part of the Lord's plan for humanity.

> ***Acts 2:14-16*** *But Peter, taking his stand with the eleven, raised his voice and declared to them: "Men of Judea and all you who live in Jerusalem, let this be known to you and give heed to my words. "For these men are not drunk, as you suppose, for it is only the third hour of the day; but this is what was spoken of through the prophet Joel…*

Briefly, we will see here again that the Day of YHWH is flexible in its use. In his sermon at Pentecost, Peter clearly states that what the audience is witnessing is the DOY taking place. The interesting part is that in 2 Thessalonians, Paul just as clearly (and actually more strongly), states that the DOY has *not* arrived yet. This need not derail us or concern us. Jesus said that Elijah's return as predicted by Malachi was fulfilled by John the Baptizer. This implies that the DOY was being fulfilled then, too. It is already established as precedent in the Old Testament that the DOY happens *within* history as a type, and it *ends* history in its ultimate fulfillment. So in this case Peter is clearly using DOY as a type here. Put another way, there can be *a* day of the LORD, vs. *THE* Day of the LORD.

Having said that, we will now see that all the following references will point to a clear conclusion: that both Jesus and Paul not only retained the Old Testament motif of the DOY, but they both modified it to be in reference to Jesus Himself.

> ***Luke 17:22-25*** *And He said to the disciples, "The days will come when you will long to see one of the days of the Son of Man, and you will not see it. 23 "They will say to you, 'Look there! Look here!' Do not go away, and do not run after them. 24 "For just like the lightning, when it flashes out of one part of the sky, shines to the other part of the sky, so will the Son of Man be* ***in His day****."*

Here, Jesus is clearly talking about His return at the end of history (but this is debated, as we will see in chapter 7). He does not say the "Day of the Lord" but it is plainly clear that He means it that way. His point is that the Day of Jesus Christ will not be long and drawn out, but quick and instantaneous, so therefore they should not expect to engage Him in interaction. If anyone says that he is Jesus returning, they must be lying.

> ***1 Corinthians 5:4-5*** *I have decided to deliver such a one to Satan for the destruction of his flesh, so that his spirit may be saved in* ***the day of the Lord Jesus****.*

In what must be one of the earliest New Testament passages, we see that Paul has the same thing in mind as Jesus: the DOY is now to be 're-wrapped' in the person of Jesus. This is important to demonstrate the continuity of scripture on this subject, but more importantly, *it speaks volumes on Whom Paul considered Jesus to be!* Changing the term "Day of Yahweh" to "Day of Jesus the Messiah" was not a flippant or casual change of wording for Paul; it means that Paul viewed Jesus of Nazareth to be the embodiment of Yahweh of Israel. The Day of the Lord was proclaimed by Yahweh in the Old Testament; that same God was now revealed in the form of Jesus, and now He too was proclaiming "His" day.

> ***Philippians 1:6*** *For I am confident of this very thing, that He who began a good work in you will perfect it until* ***the day of Christ Jesus****.*

Lest we think that the previous reference is a fluke, we see Paul use the term again: the day of Christ Jesus. The warnings and promises regarding the DOY are still in effect via the person of Jesus of Nazareth. This is a bold theological claim.

1 Thessalonians 5:1-10 *Now as to the times and the epochs, brethren, you have no need of anything to be written to you. 2 For you yourselves know full well that* ***the day of the Lord*** *will come just like a thief in the night. 3 While they are saying, "Peace and safety!" then destruction will come upon them suddenly like labor pains upon a woman with child, and they will not escape. 4 But you, brethren, are not in darkness, that the day would overtake you like a thief; 5 for you are all sons of light and sons of day. We are not of night nor of darkness; 6 so then let us not sleep as others do, but let us be alert and sober. 7 For those who sleep do their sleeping at night, and those who get drunk get drunk at night. 8 But since we are of the day, let us be sober, having put on the breastplate of faith and love, and as a helmet, the hope of salvation. 9 For God has not destined us for wrath, but for obtaining salvation through our Lord Jesus Christ, 10 who died for us, so that whether we are awake or asleep, we will live together with Him.*

It seems that the people in the church of Thessalonica took the DOY seriously. They were abuzz with the worry that they might have missed it, but Paul sets them straight and says it is still far off in the future. A couple of things to note here. First, there is the clear statement of destruction which is entirely in keeping with the Old Testament mindset, while there is a note of comfort for believers as being 'sons of light.' Once again, as in the DOY, there is the double edged sword of destruction/deliverance.

Secondly, there is a clear statement that the believer should not be caught off guard, but should see the day coming. This is an interesting contrast to the idea that nobody knows when Jesus will return. Jesus did say nobody knows the day or the hour, but He also indicated that God's people should be able to read the times (Matt. 16:1-4). Likewise, Paul here shows an expectation that his students will not be caught off guard.

> ***2 Thessalonians 2:1-10*** *Now we request you, brethren, with regard to* ***the coming of our Lord Jesus Christ*** *and our gathering together to Him, 2 that you not be quickly shaken from your composure or be disturbed either by a spirit or a message or a letter as if from us, to the effect that* ***the day of the Lord*** *has come. 3 Let no one in any way deceive you, for* <u>*it will not come unless*</u> *the apostasy comes first, and the man of lawlessness is revealed, the son of destruction, 4 who opposes and exalts himself above every so-called god or object of worship, so that he takes his seat in the temple of God, displaying himself as being God. 5 Do you not remember that while I was still with you, I was telling you these things? 6 And you know what restrains him now, so that in his time he will be revealed. 7 For the mystery of lawlessness is already at work; only he who now restrains will do so until he is taken out of the way. 8 Then that lawless one will be revealed* <u>*whom the Lord will slay*</u> *with the breath of His mouth and bring to an end by the appearance of His coming; 9 that is, the one whose coming is in accord with the activity of Satan, with all power and signs and false wonders, 10 and with all the deception of wickedness for those who perish, because they did not receive the love of the truth so as to be saved.*

As mentioned before, we now see the contrast between

Peter and Paul. Peter said that Pentecost was a type of the DOY; here, Paul says that the Day of the Lord certainly has *not* come, and furthermore, *will not come* until other things have taken place. Notice again, that just as the Old Testament forewarns of the destruction of the wicked, so will Jesus slay the man of lawlessness.

> ***2Peter 3:10-13*** *But **the day of the Lord** will come like a thief, in which the heavens will pass away with a roar and the elements will be destroyed with intense heat, and the earth and its works will be burned up. 11 Since all these things are to be destroyed in this way, what sort of people ought you to be in holy conduct and godliness, 12 looking for and hastening the coming of **the day of God**, because of which the heavens will be destroyed by burning, and the elements will melt with intense heat! 13 But according to His promise we are looking for new heavens and a new earth, in which righteousness dwells.*

Jesus said that He would return like a thief in the night; here Peter says that the Day of the Lord will come like a thief. Once again, we see how the DOY becomes a statement of the deity of Jesus: Jesus will return like a thief, *therefore,* the day of the Lord will be in like manner. Once again, the destructive element is involved as well.

We've established a clear link between the Old Testament Day of YHWH and Jesus of Nazareth. The DOY is now the Day Of Jesus Christ (DOJC). We've established that the Old Testament idea of the DOY is not only still in effect, it is a vital piece of the unfolding of history. Now that we have that done, we can include other statements which reinforce what we've learned. In the following section, we will see the DOJC implied in various statements.

> ***Matthew 7:21-23*** *" Not everyone who says to Me, 'Lord, Lord,' will enter the kingdom of heaven, but he who does the will of My Father who is in heaven will enter. 22 " Many will say to Me* <u>*on that day*</u>*, 'Lord, Lord, did we not prophesy in Your name, and in Your name cast out demons, and in Your name perform many miracles?' 23 "And then I will declare to them, 'I never knew you; depart from me, you who practice lawlessness.'"*

The setting is very clear: Jesus is talking about a day of judgment, which of course, is what the Old Testament repeatedly said the DOY was. In this case, though, Jesus says that *He* will be the one judging people and deciding their fate. Just as Amos warned Israel that the DOY will not bring comfort to them, Jesus here warns false followers that the judgment *in that day* will not be beneficial to them, either.

> ***Matthew 24:36/Mark 13:32*** *"But of* <u>*that day*</u> *and hour no one knows, not even the angels of heaven, nor the Son, but the Father alone. 37 "For* <u>*the coming of the Son of Man*</u> *will be just like the days of Noah."*

Jesus is speaking of His return (though some dispute this), and notice His use of *that day*. Sometimes 'that day' is a casual reference to a point in time ("that day, Jesus went into the boat..."); sometimes though, 'that day' means THAT DAY, and this is the case here. "That day" means the DOJC, and we now see that this also means

His return. In the next chapter, we will see later that Paul takes the DOY/DOJC to mean just that as well.

Luke 10:12 *"I say to you, it will be more tolerable in that day for Sodom than for that city."*

Here Jesus is condemning His countryman for being so hard-hearted. "That day" clearly means a day of judgment, and their verdict will not be favorable. In a sense, Jesus continues the long tradition of the Old Testament Jewish prophets warning God's people of their impending doom.

Luke 21:25-28; 34-35 *"There will be signs in sun and moon and stars, and on the earth dismay among nations, in perplexity at the roaring of the sea and the waves, 26 men fainting from fear and the expectation of the things which are coming upon the world; for the powers of the heavens will be shaken. Then they will see the Son of Man coming in a cloud with power and great glory. 28 "But when these things begin to take place, straighten up and lift up your heads, because your redemption is drawing near."*

34 " Be on guard, so that your hearts will not be weighted down with dissipation and drunkenness and the worries of life, and that day will not come on you suddenly like a trap; 35 for it will come upon all those who dwell on the face of all the earth. 36 "But keep on the alert at all times, praying that you may have strength to escape all these things that are about to take place, and to stand before the Son of Man."

The context once again merges the Day of the Lord (That Day) with the return of Jesus. Notice that here,

Jesus (like Paul) says that they should have some anticipation of His return. There is the added exhortation to keep diligent in their spiritual devotion, and like Zephaniah, warns of global judgment.

> ***2Thessalonians 1:6-11*** *For after all it is only just for God to repay with affliction those who afflict you, 7 and to give relief to you who are afflicted and to us as well when the Lord Jesus will be revealed from heaven with His mighty angels in flaming fire, 8 dealing out retribution to those who do not know God and to those who do not obey the gospel of our Lord Jesus. 9 These will pay the penalty of eternal destruction, away from the presence of the Lord and from the glory of His power, 10 when He comes to be glorified in His saints* **on that day**, *and to be marveled at among all who have believed — for our testimony to you was believed.*

In a very short space, Paul expresses all the components of the DOJC: On *that day*, Jesus will return, and deal out retribution, resulting in eternal destruction. This is in complete accord with the Old Testament concept of the DOY: God returns, punishes and destroys the wicked while providing comfort to His own.

> ***2 Timothy 1:12*** *For this reason I also suffer these things, but I am not ashamed; for I know whom I have believed and I am convinced that He is able to guard what I have entrusted to Him until that day.*

"That day" is obviously the DOJC: Paul is saying that his hope for salvation is in the hands of Jesus.

2 Timothy 1:15-18 *The Lord grant mercy to the house of Onesiphorus, for he often refreshed me and was not ashamed of my chains; 17 but when he was in Rome, he eagerly searched for me and found me — 18 the Lord grant to him to find mercy from the Lord on that day — and you know very well what services he rendered at Ephesus.*

Paul basically prays that Onesiphorus, a devoted fellow believer will find mercy "on that day." The implication is clear that the day in question is one of judgment.

2 Timothy 4:8 *… in the future there is laid up for me the crown of righteousness, which the Lord, the righteous Judge, will award to me on that day; and not only to me, but also to all who have loved His appearing.*

Once again we see the other side of the judgment day: the day of rewards for God's people. The promise of rewards is Paul's hope after a long ministry of suffering and trial, and in particular, facing death as he is here. "His appearing" could refer to the past earthly life of Jesus, or the appearing that is in conjunction with the DOJC.

Having established the expectations for "That day", we can see it referred to in other places:

John 6:39 *"This is the will of Him who sent Me, that of all that He has given Me I lose nothing, but raise it up on* ***the last day****".*

John 6:40 *"For this is the will of My Father, that everyone who beholds the Son and believes in Him will have eternal life, and I Myself will raise him up on* ***the last day****."*

> ***John 6:44*** *"No one can come to Me unless the Father who sent Me draws him; and I will raise him up on* ***the last day****.*
>
> ***John 6:54*** *"He who eats My flesh and drinks My blood has eternal life, and I will raise him up on* ***the last day****.*
>
> ***John 11:24*** *Martha said to Him, "I know that he will rise again in the resurrection on* ***the last day****."*

All of these can be taken together: each verse states that Jesus will resurrect His deceased followers on "*the last day*". Notice, that in the story from John 11, Martha already has the expectation of a resurrection on "the last day". In fact, her hope is that Lazarus will *at that time* be resurrected. Instead, Jesus raises Lazarus immediately as a proto-type of the future resurrection.

A great question to ask here is this: why is the term 'last day' used? Simple: because the ultimate Day of the Lord is the day that ENDS history. As such, it is the last day of This Age. This fits perfectly within the Old Testament and New Testament framework of the Day of the Lord.

Notice in the next reference:

> ***John 12:48*** *"He who rejects Me and does not receive My sayings, has one who judges him; the word I spoke is what will judge him at* ***the last day****."*

All the previous references made note of resurrection on the last day; in this verse, the last day is one of *judgment.* Thus the double edge meaning of DOY is retained: it is a day of judgment and deliverance both.

We have other collaborative evidence for this view.

Jesus used yet another phrase to speak of this day: the end of the age.

> ***Matthew 13:39, 40****... and the enemy who sowed them is the devil, and the harvest is the* ***end of the age****; and the reapers are angels. "So just as the tares are gathered up and burned with fire, so shall it be at the* ***end of the age****.*
>
> ***Matthew 13:49*** *"So it will be at the* ***end of the age****; the angels will come forth and take out the wicked from among the righteous..."*
>
> ***Matthew 24:3*** *As He was sitting on the Mount of Olives, the disciples came to Him privately, saying, "Tell us, when will these things happen, and what will be the sign of Your coming, and of the* ***end of the age****?"*
>
> ***Matthew 28:20*** *"... teaching them to observe all that I commanded you; and lo, I am with you always, even to the* ***end of the age****."*

"End of the age" fits in perfectly with the whole premise of this book: the Biblical view of unfolding history is This Age / The Day of the Lord / The Age to Come. In these passages, Jesus says that at the end of the age there will be judgment. We have already seen that He warns of judgment upon His return. The great judgment is the day of the Lord's return which is the Day of Christ Jesus which is the Day of Yahweh which is the Last Day which is the End of the Age. Furthermore, notice that in Matthew 13:49, it says the wicked will be removed *from* the righteous, as opposed to the righteous being brought someplace else for safety.

DAY OF YHWH / DAY OF CHRIST JESUS / DAY OF JUDGMENT

In my experience, few things have been overlooked as much as the idea of judgment day. It is found in everyday speech, even amongst non-Christians, but in our theology, we don't say much about it. Because we've been caught up in the idea of Rapture and are captive to faulty theology, we really don't know what to do with Judgment Day, but it's prevalent in the New Testament, so we should have something to say about it.

I offer the following verses to demonstrate that Judgment Day was heavily present in the thinking of Jesus and the early Apostles. Rather than comment on each one, I will let them speak for themselves, simply to show that this is not a whim or some theological sideshow. It should have a prominent place in our eschatology.

Matthew 10:15 *"Truly I say to you, it will be more tolerable for the land of Sodom and Gomorrah in* ***the day of judgment*** *than for that city."*

Matthew 11:22 *"Nevertheless I say to you, it will be more tolerable for Tyre and Sidon in* ***the day of judgment*** *than for you."*

Matthew 11:24 *"Nevertheless I say to you that it will be more tolerable for the land of Sodom in* ***the day of judgment****, than for you."*

Matthew 12:36 *"But I tell you that every careless word that people speak, they shall give an accounting for it in* ***the day of judgment****.*

Matthew 12:41 *"The men of Nineveh will stand up with this generation at the* ***judgment****, and will condemn it because they repented at the preaching of Jonah; and behold, something greater than Jonah is here.*

Matthew 12:42 *"The Queen of the South will rise up with this generation at the* ***judgment*** *and will condemn it, because she came from the ends of the earth to hear the wisdom of Solomon; and behold, something greater than Solomon is here."*

John 5:22 *"For not even the Father judges anyone, but He has given all* ***judgment*** *to the Son…"*

John 5:29 *and will come forth; those who did the good deeds to a resurrection of life, those who committed the evil deeds to a resurrection of* ***judgment"****.*

John 12:31 *"Now* ***judgment*** *is upon this world; now the ruler of this world will be cast out.*

John 16:8 *"And He, when He comes, will convict the world concerning sin and righteousness and* ***judgment****;"*

Acts 24:25 *But as he was discussing righteousness, self-control and the* ***judgment*** *to come, Felix became frightened and said, "Go away for the present, and when I find time I will summon you."*

Romans 2:3 *But do you suppose this, O man, when you pass* ***judgment*** *on those who practice such things and do the same yourself, that you will escape the* ***judgment of God?***

Romans 2:5 *But because of your stubbornness and unrepentant heart you are storing up wrath for yourself in the* *day of wrath and revelation of the righteous* ***judgment*** *of God,*

Romans 14:*10 But you, why do you judge your brother? Or you again, why do you regard your brother with contempt? For we will all stand before the* ***judgment*** *seat of God.*

2 Corinthians 5:10 *For we must all appear before the* ***judgment*** *seat of Christ, so that each one may be recompensed for his deeds in the body, according to what he has done, whether good or bad.*

1 Timothy 5:24 *The sins of some men are quite evident, going before them to* ***judgment****; for others, their sins follow after.*

Hebrews 9:27 *And inasmuch as it is appointed for men to die once and after this comes* ***judgment****,*

Hebrews 10:27 *but a terrifying expectation of* ***judgment*** *and the fury of a fire which will consume the adversaries.*

James 2:13 *For* ***judgment*** *will be merciless to one who has shown no mercy; mercy triumphs over* ***judgment****.*

1 Peter 4:17 *For it is time for* ***judgment*** *to begin with the household of God; and if it begins with us first, what will be the outcome for those who do not obey the gospel of God?*

2 Peter 2:*4 For if God did not spare angels when they sinned, but cast them into hell and committed them to pits of darkness, reserved for* ***judgment****;*

2 Peter 2:9 *then the Lord knows how to rescue the godly from temptation, and to keep the unrighteous under punishment for* ***the day of judgment****,*

2 Peter 3:7 *But by His word the present heavens and earth* *are being reserved for fire, kept for* ***the day of judgment*** *and destruction of ungodly men.*

1 John 4:17 *By this, love is perfected with us, so that we may have confidence in* ***the day of judgment****; because as He is, so also are we in this world.*

Jude 6 *And angels who did not keep their own domain, but abandoned their proper abode, He has kept in eternal bonds under darkness for the* ***judgment*** *of the great day,*

SUMMARY

There's not much room for any doubt about the matter. The Day Of the Lord, which the Old Testament prophets predicted and warned about, still had currency in the New Testament church. Here are the key points from this chapter:

First, the term "Day of the Lord" was still in use by the New Testament writers and early church. It had not passed from the parlance of God's people.

Second, both Jesus and Paul re-oriented the DOY so that it revolved around Jesus Himself. Jesus assumes the role of judge, just as Yahweh did in the Old Testament, and refers to it being HIS day. Paul takes the DOY and begins speaking of the "Day of Jesus Christ" without any contradiction to his monotheistic belief. This is a major step in how Jesus is perceived by both Himself and His followers: nobody can take the place of Yahweh, the God of Israel, but Jesus and Paul take one of the foundational concepts about God, the Day of Yahweh, and begin using it as the Day of Christ Jesus.

Third, the aspects of the DOY which the Old Testament brought forth, judgment and deliverance are still both present in the DOJC. Judgment involves destruction or deliverance to life with the Lord Jesus.

Fourth, the return of Jesus is clearly pegged to the Day of the Lord / Day of Jesus Christ. The DOY was often depicted in the Old Testament as God visiting His people for judgment. Jesus is spoken of in the same manner, that He will return, and in this return there will be retribution for the wicked, and salvation for His people.

Fifth, the Day of the Lord is also known as the Last Day because it ends This Age. Whenever Jesus speaks of the Last Day, it has elements of both judgment and deliverance.

Everything that was foreboding and frightful about the Old Testament DOY is still in effect; everything that was comforting is still in effect. Those who would divide up the Bible into the "mean" Old Testament God and the "nice" New Testament God (and Jesus) are not paying close attention to the scripture. All humanity has a day of judgment hanging over its head, and the grace and love of Jesus includes this frightening idea. There is no break between "mean" and "nice" testaments here.

7

The Return of Jesus

This subject was already introduced in the last chapter. The premise of this book makes it impossible to completely keep such subjects separated. We learned how the New Testament retained the Old Testament idea of the Day of the Lord and transformed it into the Day of Jesus Christ. Part of that transformation involves the Lord's promise to return to earth, so we have to touch upon it.

In this chapter, we will focus on just that aspect of the Lord's return. This is perhaps the most discussed topic of Christian circles: "When will Jesus return, if at all?" Some say it's a metaphor, some say it's fulfilled in other ways, and some say it will happen at any time, and others say some events must take place first. Entire books are written on this subject for which this one chapter will need to suffice.

As we study this topic in particular, we will see that

the main passages that we consult have already been referenced. The reason is simple: the concepts are so intertwined that the one idea (Day of Christ Jesus) involves the other (the Return of Jesus). When we study the resurrection we will see this again.

One important note before we look at the passages: when forming our theology, *we need to start with what is clearly stated and fill in from there*. Unfortunately, when it comes to this subject, people usually do the opposite: they start with the most ambiguous, mystical and metaphorical verses first, and then ignore what is plainly stated. Case in point, most people begin with Revelation to explore this topic, which is not a good idea. It would be like studying the Temple of Jerusalem and reading Ezekiel 40 & 41 first. That passage is highly symbolic and mystical, and says nothing about the actual temple of Solomon or Herod.

In this case, although I will reference Revelation later (and already have), we will begin in other places. We have already seen and will explore again that Paul speaks very plainly on this subject: *The day of Christ Jesus is the day of His return, and of the resurrection and of judgment.*

Just as the Old Testament depicts the DOY as being judgment and deliverance, or destruction, the DOJC has the same aspects. The only difference is that they are fleshed out with the teachings on the Lord's return and our resurrection. This is written plain as day, and we will let scripture speak for itself.

A Definite Promise Of Jesus' Return

In case anybody raises the basic issue of whether Jesus made a promise to return, it will be establish here that Jesus both taught this idea and that the early church believed it.

Matthew 24:25-27 *"Behold, I have told you in advance. 26 "So if they say to you, 'Behold, He is in the wilderness,' do not go out, or, 'Behold, He is in the inner rooms,' do not believe them. 27 "For just as the lightning comes from the east and flashes even to the west, so will the coming of the Son of Man be."*

Matthew 24:36-41 *"But of that day and hour no one knows, not even the angels of heaven, nor the Son, but the Father alone. 37 "For the coming of the Son of Man will be just like the days of Noah. 38 "For as in those days before the flood they were eating and drinking, marrying and giving in marriage, until the day that Noah entered the ark, 39 and they did not understand until the flood came and took them all away; so will the coming of the Son of Man be. 40 "Then there will be two men in the field; one will be taken and one will be left. 41 "Two women will be grinding at the mill; one will be taken and one will be left."*

There's some ambiguity about what Jesus is trying to convey here. On the one hand, He seems to be predicting one very specific point: His return will be very quick with no time to mull things over. On the other hand, there are good reasons to interpret passages like this to be referring to the fall of Jerusalem in 70AD. False messiahs were frequent in the Biblical era; having seen this, Jesus took pains to make sure there would be no uncertainty about someone claiming to be Him returning. Life will continue on as normal, just as it did in Noah's day, and then there will be a deluge of judgment concurrent with His return.

Luke 18:8 *"I tell you that He will bring about justice for them quickly. However, when the Son of Man comes, will He find faith on the earth?"*

The context is a parable about praying steadfastly and being diligent over a long period of time. Although not specifically stated outright, the implication is that His return is far off. The pretext of the parable is persistence, and Jesus' warning is to keep waiting in watchfulness despite the late hour.

John 14:3-4 *"If I go and prepare a place for you,* ***I will come again*** *and receive you to Myself, that where I am, there you may be also."*

John 14:18-19 *"I will not leave you as orphans;* ***I will come to you****."*

John 14:28 *"You heard that I said to you, 'I go away,* ***and I will come to you****.' If you loved Me, you would have rejoiced because I go to the Father, for the Father is greater than I."*

Three times in one chapter, Jesus promises a return. He is at the beginning of His Passion, soon to be arrested. I suppose someone could claim that His promise to return is fulfilled by the Resurrection, but the tone doesn't allow it. When He speaks of going to the Father, it is not in His death and resurrection but in His ascension, and after this He will return.

Acts 1:10-11 *And as they were gazing intently into the sky while He was going, behold, two men in white clothing stood beside them. 11 They also said, "Men of Galilee, why do you stand looking into the sky? This Jesus, who has been taken up from you into heaven, will come in just the same way as you have watched Him go into heaven."*

Here we have a third party repeating Jesus' promise, after the ascension. An angel declares that they will see Him again in a observable way, just as He departed.

1 Corinthians 11:26 *For as often as you eat this bread and drink the cup, you proclaim the Lord's death until He comes.*

In his instructions on how to conduct the Lord's supper, Paul casually refers to the Lord's return without any explanation or attempt to bolster his argument. The idea is decided and settled that the Lord *will* return. Being that he did not elaborate on the issue, it seems to have been assumed by his audience.

1 Corinthians 15:23-25 *But each in his own order: Christ the first fruits, after that those who are Christ's at His coming, 24 then comes the end, when He hands over the kingdom to the God and Father, when He has abolished all rule and all authority and power.*

We will explore 1 Corinthians 15 in detail later, but briefly, an interesting note: this entire chapter concerns the resurrection. Because the Lord's return and the resurrection are overlapping events, by necessity, he must also talk about the return of Christ.

1 Timothy 6:14-15 *...that you keep the commandment without stain or reproach until the appearing of our Lord Jesus Christ, 15 which He will bring about at the proper time.*

Once again, without explanation or effort to clarify the situation, Paul casually mentions the return of Christ.

Hebrews 9:27-28 *And inasmuch as it is appointed for men to die once and after this comes* ***judgment****, 28 so Christ also, having been offered once to bear the sins of many, will appear a second time for salvation without reference to sin, to those who eagerly await Him.*

The author of Hebrews without being obvious about it, links the judgment of humanity with the return of Jesus.

Matthew 25:31-33 *But when the Son of Man comes in His glory, and all the angels with Him, then He will sit on His glorious throne. 32 "All the nations will be gathered before Him; and He will separate them from one another, as the shepherd separates the sheep from the goats; 33 and He will put the sheep on His right, and the goats on the left.*

Here, Jesus once again makes a clear reference to his eventual return, and just as the DOY often depicts the universal gathering of humanity for judgment, Jesus does so here in the context of His return and His role in that judgment. Once again we see the overlapping of the DOY, the return of Jesus, and judgment.

The Timing of the Return of Jesus

We've established now the clear expectation of the

Lord's return. Jesus, Paul and Peter proclaimed this promise to their followers. Now the question needs to be asked: "When will this happen?" In phrasing it this way, I don't mean to suggest or believe that we can find or pick the date in the future when it will happen. We can't. But in the Biblical timeline of unfolding history, we can establish at least where it falls in the time frame. Paul says it quite plainly in 1 and 2 Thessalonians.

> ***1 Thessalonians 4:13-5:2*** *But we do not want you to be uninformed, brethren, about those who are asleep, so that you will not grieve as do the rest who have no hope. 14 For if we believe that Jesus died and rose again, even so God will bring with Him those who have fallen asleep in Jesus. 15 For this we say to you by the word of the Lord, that we who are alive and remain* ***until the coming of the Lord****, will not precede those who have fallen asleep. 16 For* ***the Lord Himself will descend from heaven*** *with a shout, with the voice of the archangel and with the trumpet of God, and the dead in Christ will rise first. 17 Then we who are alive and remain will be caught up together with them in the clouds to meet the Lord in the air, and so we shall always be with the Lord. 18 Therefore comfort one another with these words*
>
> ***5:1*** *Now as to the times and the epochs, brethren, you have no need of anything to be written to you. 2 For you yourselves know full well that the day of the Lord will come just like a thief in the night.*

We've looked at this passage before, but it is useful to see how Paul weaves together all of the strands of our study in one place. First, we've talked about deceased believers. They are 'asleep in Christ.' Second, verse 14 and 16 are clear statements about the Lord's return (notice how God is said to return, which obviously is a reference to Jesus' return). Third, the strand of resurrection is brought in, as Paul says that those who are asleep will be brought with the Lord when He returns, as they are resurrected. Fourth, at the end of this passage, Paul calls this day, the "Day of the Lord."

Notice that in accordance with Jesus' prediction that His return will be like a thief in the night, Paul says *the day of the Lord* will come like a thief in the night. The reason is simple: *the day of the Lord and the return of Jesus are the same event!*

Is it really this simple, or is this just a poorly worded passage that can be misunderstood? We have an answer: Paul phrased it again in his second letter to the Thessalonians:

> ***2 Thessalonians 2:1-2*** *Now we request you, brethren, with regard to the coming of our Lord Jesus Christ and our gathering together to Him, 2 that you not be quickly shaken from your composure or be disturbed either by a spirit or a message or a letter as if from us, to the effect that the day of the Lord has come.*

In the above letter (which was written later), Paul says it again: the coming of the Lord Jesus coincides with the Day of the Lord. Apparently, Paul's teaching was getting mangled, so he had to say it again later to clarify things. If he phrased it badly so as to be misunderstood, it would be hard to explain why he phrased it so similarly in the next round. The simple fact is this: Paul DID view the return of Jesus and the Day of the Lord to be the same event. Furthermore, there will be no need, nor time to write a letter telling them it has happened.

The matter still remains as to *when* this happens. Again, Paul is perfectly clear on the issue: It has not happened yet. This is the point that he is trying to drive home to his readers. But then he continues:

> ***2 Thessalonians 2:3-8*** *Let no one in any way deceive you, for* ***it will not come*** *unless the apostasy comes first, and the man of lawlessness is revealed, the son of destruction, 4 who opposes and exalts himself above every so-called god or object of worship, so that he takes his seat in the temple of God, displaying himself as being God. 5 Do you not remember that while I was still with you, I was telling you these things? 6 And you know what restrains him now, so that in his time he will be revealed. 7 For the mystery of lawlessness is already at work; only he who now restrains will do so until he is taken out of the way. 8 Then that lawless one will be revealed whom the Lord will slay with the breath of His mouth and bring to an end by the appearance of His coming;*

Paul seems to point to a specific 'end of history' man who is the great and ultimate opponent of God; beyond this, we cannot pinpoint more specifically who this person is. However, this brief description does fit the traditional depiction of the antichrist figure: a singularly rebellious person who opposes God. Paul goes on to delineate the *modus operandi* of this man:

> ***2 Thessalonians 2:9-10****…that is, the one whose coming is in accord with the activity of Satan, with all power and signs and false wonders, 10 and with all the deception of wickedness for those who perish, because they did not receive the love of the truth so as to be saved.*

This description aligns with the portrayal as given by the book of Revelation: a supernaturally empowered human being who publicly and powerfully defies God and leads others in his rebellion.

In the Old Testament, God repeatedly promised/threatened the destruction of the wicked on the Day of Yahweh. Paul's statement about the Day of the Lord and His dealing with the Man of Lawlessness is in complete accord with this view. Humanity is in rebellion against God; some repent and will be delivered. Others refuse to repent and face destruction. On the DOY, when Jesus returns, the rebellion ends.

An Additional Note:

In America, a particular strain of theology regarding the return of Jesus has held sway, namely, the return of Jesus and the Rapture as based upon the book of Revelation. People get twisted up in arguments about whether the return of Jesus will be pre, mid or post tribulation. Of course, things get even more complicated when we throw the millennium into the mix. After these past few chapters, the reader might ask how this teaching meshes in with that school of thought. The answer: *it doesn't.*

As I've stated already, good theology is based upon what is clearly taught, and then filled in by the less certain elements. Popular 'Rapture theology' does the opposite: it ignores what is clearly stated and then builds a theology upon scripture passages whose meanings are vague and debatable. I realize that the Christian book market is saturated with popular books based upon Rapture theology and to avoid any uncertainty, I'll state it bluntly here: Rapture theology is a faulty misunderstanding of the whole of scripture. Having said that let us go to our summary.

Summary

First, Jesus clearly taught about His actual return to Earth. In his teachings, there is nothing to suggest that He intended some spiritual or metaphorical interpretation of these statements. Furthermore, His return is a quick moment like a flash of lightning, not a gradual or ongoing transaction that can be observed over time. Therefore, anyone who proclaims themselves to be Jesus in His return is simply lying.

Second, in speaking about His return, He included elements of both judgment and deliverance. For his followers, He says "I will not leave you as orphans," but He also says he will separate the 'goats from the sheep' and will send away evildoers. This fits entirely within the framework set up by the Old Testament.

Third, Jesus clearly equates His return with the Last Day of This Age. By default then, this equates His return with the Day of the Lord. Paul makes this an ironclad connection in 1 and 2 Thessalonians. In his writings there, Paul clearly ties the Day of the Lord with the return of Jesus and with the resurrection. *There is no mistaking this.*

Fourth, while Jesus says "No man knows the hour" of His return, Paul also says that God's people are not in darkness so they should not be caught unawares, but see the day coming. He also specifically says that the DOY has not come yet, and will not come until the "Man of Lawlessness" is revealed. So we have to strike a balance between foolishly setting a date based on mystical interpretation of verses and keeping a wary eye on the times and understanding them.

Jesus is coming back. This will be the Day of Yahweh. This will be the day of Christ Jesus. This will be the Last Day. This will be End of the Age. This will be the day of Resurrection.

And resurrection will be our next chapter…

8

Resurrection

We've touched on the subject of resurrection here and there already; it's impossible not to when the themes of the Bible are so interwoven. As we start, we will eliminate two thoughts right away. First, resurrection is *not* about us continuing on in another form immediately after death. Second, resurrection does *not* mean our souls being reinserted into our bodies at some point in the future. As we discuss the resurrection in this study, it means only one thing: the literal raising from the dead of the whole person, both body and soul.

This chapter will make the following points. First, the Old Testament has hints of a resurrection but does not elaborate upon it. Second, the New Testament plainly teaches about the resurrection, as it was already matter of belief even before the ministry of Jesus. Third, we will see that there is a differentiation between the resurrection of Jesus and the general resurrection of God's people. Fourth, we will see that the resurrection of God's people takes place in the future as a segment of the Day of the Lord.

Resurrection in the Old Testament

While the general tone of the Old Testament points to the utter end of life at death, there are few outright promises of life and/or resurrection. Mostly, we see some *hints* that something else is in store for God's people. Having said that, let's begin with the clearest and sharpest statement on the subject:

> ***Daniel 12:1-3*** *"Now at that time Michael, the great prince who stands guard over the sons of your people, will arise. And there will be a time of distress such as never occurred since there was a nation until that time; and at that time your people, everyone who is found written in the book, will be rescued. 2 "Many of those who sleep in the dust of the ground* ***will awake****, these to everlasting life, but the others to disgrace and everlasting contempt. 3 "Those who have insight will shine brightly like the brightness of the expanse of heaven, and those who lead the many to righteousness, like the stars forever and ever."*

No other Old Testament passage has this kind of clarity on the subject, but we will find that the other statements align with it pretty well. Important parallels can be seen with what we've already discussed. First, Jesus predicted His return after some great tribulation on earth. Second, we've established that the Day of the Lord is the

Day of Christ Jesus, which includes His return and the resurrection. What do we see here? First there will be great distress, *and then* there will be a resurrection unto life or disgrace. This completely aligns with what we've already covered. It also reinforces the concept of 'asleep in Christ'.

Because this statement is so clear, I began with it, so as to use it as a template for all that follows.

> ***2 Samuel 14:14*** *"For we will surely die and are like water spilled on the ground which cannot be gathered up again. Yet God does not take away life, but plans ways so that the banished one will not be cast out from him."*

This passage is perhaps the earliest writing we have on the idea of resurrection, and it is rather vague. It comes from a woman speaking to King David as an advocate for his banished son, Absalom. It is rather irrelevant to her plea, but it states that at death, life is really over, and then goes on with a 'But wait!' moment. God plans ways around death she says, without elaborating on what she means.

> ***Psalm 16:10-11*** *For You will not abandon my soul to Sheol;*
>
> *Nor will You allow Your Holy One to undergo decay.*
>
> *11 You will make known to me the path of life; In Your presence is fullness of joy;*
>
> *In Your right hand there are pleasures forever.*

This passage is central in Peter's sermon at Pentecost, and he uses it squarely in reference to Jesus as Messiah.

Whether it should be interpreted only for Jesus or for God's people in general is secondary to our immediate concern. The main point is that life after death is promised in some form, and therefore points to resurrection.

> ***Psalm 49:14-15*** *As sheep they are appointed for* ***Sheol;*** *Death shall be their shepherd;*
>
> *And the upright shall rule over them in the morning,*
>
> *And their form shall be for* ***Sheol*** *to consume so that they have no habitation.*
>
> *15 But God will redeem my soul from the power of Sheol for He will receive me.*

Both aspects of resurrection are pointed at here along the lines of Daniel. First is the destructive nature of Sheol. All of verse 14 is about the complete cessation of existence for the wicked. This aligns with the standard point of view of the Old Testament: the wicked are always designated as heading for destruction. Secondly, the twist here is that the writer expects better things for himself: he will be redeemed from Sheol, just as in Psalm 16. Again, this is a hint of resurrection.

> ***Psalm 73:23-28*** *Nevertheless I am continually with You; You have taken hold of my right hand.*
>
> *24 With Your counsel You will guide me, and afterward receive me to glory.*
>
> *25 Whom have I in heaven but You? And besides You, I desire nothing on earth.*
>
> *26 My flesh and my heart may fail, but God is the strength of my heart and my portion forever.*

27 For, behold, those who are far from You will perish;
You have destroyed all those who are unfaithful to You.
28 But as for me, the nearness of God is my good; I have made the Lord GOD my refuge, that I may tell of all Your works.

In this Psalm, which laments how the wicked get ahead while the righteous suffer, the turning point comes when the Psalmist recalls what the end of the wicked will be. He has hope for justice, not in this age, but in the next. He will be received by God into glory, but *the wicked will perish.* The meaning and the ramifications could not be clearer: the wicked perish and are destroyed, not in this life but in the next. That is the whole foundation of his hope, not justice in the here and now.

Isaiah 24:21-23 *So it will happen in that day,*
That the LORD will punish the host of heaven on high,
And the kings of the earth on earth.
22 They will be gathered together like prisoners in the dungeon,
And will be confined in prison; And after many days they will be punished.
23 Then the moon will be abashed and the sun ashamed,
For the LORD of hosts will reign on Mount Zion and in Jerusalem,
And His glory will be before His elders.

This passage falls into place with the point of view that Sheol/Hades is just a "holding tank" until the judgment day. First, notice the phrase "In that day" which is a signal to the DOY. Second, there is the theme of being held like a prisoner in a cell who is awaiting trial. Third, there is finally the execution of judgment. This aligns with Daniel 12 as our template, and with what is still to come in this chapter.

> ***Isaiah 25:6-9*** *The LORD of hosts will prepare a lavish banquet for all peoples on this mountain;*
>
> *A banquet of aged wine, choice pieces with marrow, and refined, aged wine.*
>
> *7 And on this mountain He will swallow up the covering which is over all peoples,*
>
> *Even the veil which is stretched over all nations.*
>
> *8 He will swallow up death for all time,*
>
> *And the Lord GOD will wipe tears away from all faces,*
>
> *And He will remove the reproach of His people from all the earth; For the LORD has spoken.*
>
> *9 And it will be said* **in that day**,
>
> *"Behold, this is our God for whom we have waited that He might save us.*
>
> *This is the LORD for whom we have waited; Let us rejoice and be glad in His salvation."*

This is a prime example of figurative language for The Age to Come. The idea of a banquet for all people is obviously a picture of paradise. In verse 7, the word 'covering' is better translated as 'shroud'; thus it is a statement about death being overturned. This is immediately reinforced by verse 8. In verse 9, there is the key phrase, "In that day." Without specifying it, the crowds giving the great proclamation of fulfilled hope are those who have risen in the resurrection unto life.

> ***Isaiah 26:14, 19-21*** *The dead will not live, the departed spirits will not rise;*
>
> *Therefore You have punished and destroyed them,*
>
> *And You have wiped out all remembrance of them.*
>
> *19 Your dead will live; Their corpses will rise. You who lie in the dust, awake and shout for joy,*
>
> *For your dew is as the dew of the dawn, And the earth will give birth to the departed spirits.*
>
> *20 Come, my people, enter into your rooms And close your doors behind you;*
>
> *Hide for a little while until indignation runs its course.*
>
> *21 For behold, the LORD is about to come out from His place to punish the inhabitants of the earth for their iniquity;*
>
> *And the earth will reveal her bloodshed and will no longer cover her slain.*

This two part section has two different targets. The first target is the wicked, who are warned that they will have no life. This will be their punishment and destruction. Then a second target: "*Your* dead" is in reference to God and His people. HIS dead will live. Notice that the place of their renewal unto life is on earth. We will see that this fits the vision of the New Jerusalem coming down from heaven in Revelation 22.

> ***Isaiah 66:15-17*** *15 For behold, the LORD will come in fire And His chariots like the whirlwind, To render His anger with fury, and His rebuke with flames of fire. 16 For the LORD will execute judgment by fire and by His sword on all flesh, and those slain by the LORD will be many. 17 "Those who sanctify and purify themselves to go to the gardens, Following one in the center, Who eat swine's flesh, detestable things and mice, will come to an end altogether," declares the LORD.*

The larger context of this passage is clearly of an apocalyptic nature. The chapter follows a long series of promises about a heavenly Jerusalem, which will nourish God's children. Then the scene changes to the punishment of those who afflict them, and how God will destroy them utterly. As we will see in the next passage, a greater, happier promise is then extended to God's people.

> ***Isaiah 66:22-24*** *"For just as the new heavens and the new earth*
>
> *Which I make will endure before Me," declares the LORD,*
>
> *"So your offspring and your name will endure.*
>
> *23 "And it shall be from new moon to new moon and from sabbath to sabbath,*
>
> *All mankind will come to bow down before Me," says the LORD.*
>
> *24 "Then they will go forth and look on the corpses of the men*
>
> *Who have transgressed against Me. For their worm will not die*
>
> *And their fire will not be quenched; and they will be an abhorrence to all mankind."*

Forming the conclusion of the book of Isaiah, this passage

is a very telling overview of Old Testament expectations. The wicked are destroyed and the righteous receive the privilege of seeing justice being executed. The context is very clear that this is not about something within history but at its end. This is how Isaiah sees the closing of the story of humanity.

Ezekiel 37:11-14 *Then He said to me, "Son of man, these bones are the whole house of Israel; behold, they say, 'Our bones are dried up and our hope has perished. We are completely cut off.' 12 "Therefore prophesy and say to them, 'Thus says the Lord GOD, "Behold, I will open your graves and cause you to come up out of your graves, My people; and I will bring you into the land of Israel. 13 "Then you will know that I am the LORD, when I have opened your graves and caused you to come up out of your graves, My people. 14 "I will put My Spirit within you and you will come to life, and I will place you on your own land. Then you will know that I, the LORD, have spoken and done it," declares the LORD.'"*

This passage wraps up Ezekiel's prediction that Israel will be 'resurrected' as a people after the exile. The language seems to point to a metaphorical sense, not a literal one. However, it does illustrate another trace of resurrection within the Old Testament.

Resurrection as a Held Belief in the New Testament

If someone supposes that Jesus introduced the idea of resurrection with His teachings, they are wrong. In the period between the Old and New Testaments, there seems to have developed a clearer belief in the idea. In the story of the Maccabbean revolt, a mother exhorts her sons to sacrifice their lives for Israel, for they shall receive their lives back (2 Maccabees 7).

Within the gospels, we see that the ideas regarding resurrection are already underway, without having any input from Jesus. It is clear that the concept of resurrection had already been developing previous to His ministry. Having said that, let's begin there.

> ***Matthew 22:23*** *On that day some Sadducees (who say there is no resurrection) came to Jesus and questioned Him…*

This passage, which is paralleled in Mark 12 and Luke 20, shows the Sadducees coming to mockingly test Jesus. As we will see later in Acts, we know that there was a division between them and the Pharisees, who held to a belief in a resurrection. Jesus also held to a belief in the resurrection, as we will see later. The point of this passage is to illustrate that talk of resurrection was already in the air in Jesus' day.

> ***John 11:24*** *Martha said to Him, "I know that he will rise again* ***in the resurrection*** *on the last day."*

Here, we get two for one: First, we see that Martha already had a belief in resurrection without reference to Jesus Himself, and second, that she expected the end of history on the last day, which would be the Day of the Lord. This lines up with Jesus' promise to raise up His people *on the last day*, and with Paul's writing to the Thessalonians that the dead in Christ will rise on the Day of Christ Jesus. The difference here is that Martha did not realize that it was through Jesus that the resurrection would happen, thus Jesus' claim in verse 25 that *HE* is the resurrection.

> ***Acts 23:6-8*** *But perceiving that one group were Sadducees and the other Pharisees, Paul began crying out in the Council, " Brethren, I am a Pharisee, a son of Pharisees; I am on trial for the hope and* ***resurrection of the dead****!" 7 As he said this, there occurred a dissension between the Pharisees and Sadducees, and the assembly was divided. 8 For the Sadducees say that there is no resurrection, nor an angel, nor a spirit, but the Pharisees acknowledge them all.*

What is fascinating about this passage is that Paul paralyzes his accusers by getting them to argue about the resurrection. The debate is not about the resurrection of Jesus, but about whether there is any resurrection at all. When Pharisees heard Jesus talk about resurrection, they might have disagreed with some points of His teaching, but they would have believed with Jesus that there will be a resurrection. The Sadducees, however would have written Jesus off as one more misguided Pharisee.

Paul would find similar tension when he broached the subject in Athens on Mars Hill. The idea of resurrection would be repugnant to them, and if you read Acts 17, you can see that whenever Paul mentions resurrection, that is when the interruptions and disagreements start.

Jesus and Resurrection

We have one main focus in this section: to establish that the New Testament writers believed that Jesus of Nazareth had actually risen from the dead. Leaving aside the obvious sources of the gospels themselves, we'll look at the following passages.

> **Acts 1:21-23** *"Therefore it is necessary that of the men who have accompanied us all the time that the Lord Jesus went in and out among us — 22 beginning with the baptism of John until the day that He was taken up from us — one of these must become a witness with us of His resurrection."*

The disciples are looking for someone to take Judas' place, and the main qualification is that the candidate must have already been part of the movement. In particular, they are to have experienced the resurrection event with them. It is useful to note that out of all that they could have singled out, the chief concern was the resurrection of Jesus. The main charge against the disciples at this time is that they themselves have stolen the body of Jesus to deceive the populace; consequently, they needed someone who knew that true facts; namely that Jesus had indeed risen from the dead.

> **Acts 2:29-31** *"And so, because he was a prophet and knew that God had sworn to him with an oath to seat one of his descendents on his throne, he looked ahead and spoke of the resurrection of the Christ, that He was neither abandoned to Hades, nor did His flesh suffer decay."*

Throughout the New Testament, the followers of Jesus

repeatedly assert that the resurrection of Jesus was the fulfillment of the Old Testament writings. They include a quotation from Psalm 16. An important point needs to be made here. That there is a reference to bodily decay contradicts the idea that in speaking of a resurrection, the disciples were speaking "spiritually" or metaphorically. That the body of Jesus was raised up before it could decompose was an important point to them.

> **Acts 4:33** *And with great power the apostles were giving testimony to the resurrection of the Lord Jesus, and abundant grace was upon them all.*

Again we see that the highlight of the apostles' preaching was the resurrection of Jesus.

> **Acts 26:22-23** *"So, having obtained help from God, I stand to this day testifying both to small and great, stating nothing but what the Prophets and Moses said was going to take place; 23 that the Christ was to suffer, and that by reason of His resurrection from the dead He would be the first to proclaim light both to the Jewish people and to the Gentiles."*

In his appearance before the governor Festus, Paul is giving testimony about his old life as a persecutor of the church. Again, the only substantial content of his speech is about the resurrection of Jesus. No reference to Christ's teaching is given or of His miracles, just His resurrection. Paul says that Jesus spoke to him on the road to Damascus, which raises no conflict; but when he mentions the resurrection of Jesus, it is at *that* point that Festus interrupts Paul, calling him mad.

Romans 6:5 *For if we have become united with Him in the likeness of His death, certainly we shall also be in the likeness of* ***His resurrection...***

This is our first hint that the resurrection of Jesus has broader ramifications; namely, that because of His resurrection, we too shall be resurrected. The rite of baptism has great significance, and its purpose is borne out through the resurrection of Jesus. It can be said that baptism is the door to resurrection for Jesus' followers.

Philippians 3:9-11 *...and may be found in Him, not having a righteousness of my own derived from the Law, but that which is through faith in Christ, the righteousness which comes from God on the basis of faith, 10 that I may know Him and the power of His resurrection and the fellowship of His sufferings, being conformed to His death; 11 in order that I may attain to* ***the resurrection from the dead***.

Similar to the previous passage in Romans 6, we see the link between Christ's resurrection and that of his followers. The power of the resurrection is something *to be known*, Paul says, and this is in order to be part of another resurrection, that of Christ's followers. This reveals another important nugget: resurrection is not some mystical experience for the Christian in This Age, but is a future event. It has not happened yet. So, as we will see later in 2 Timothy, anyone who speaks of resurrection in some other way rather than as a future hope is mistaken.

> ***1 Peter 1:3-4*** *Blessed be the God and Father of our Lord Jesus Christ, who according to His great mercy has caused us to be born again to a living hope through the resurrection of Jesus Christ from the dead, 4 to obtain an inheritance which is imperishable and undefiled and will not fade away…*

Here, Peter says that the resurrection of Jesus is the agency through which believers receive the new spiritual life. Furthermore, this life leads to immortality (inheritance). Like Paul, Peter sees a link between the resurrection of Jesus and the believer's experience. This moves the Easter event beyond an historical curiosity and into the realm of contemporary spiritual attainment.

> ***1 Peter 3:21-22*** *Corresponding to that, baptism now saves you — not the removal of dirt from the flesh, but an appeal to God for a good conscience — through the resurrection of Jesus Christ, 22 who is at the right hand of God, having gone into heaven, after angels and authorities and powers had been subjected to Him.*

Like a previous passage and in line with Paul's thinking, we see the tie between baptism and resurrection. Again, baptism is the door to participation in the resurrection of Jesus. In addition to this, we see a glimpse of what Jesus went on to: ultimate universal authority at the right hand of God. Resurrection was not only the human experience of being rescued from death for Jesus, but it was the manner by which He authenticated His Lordship.

The General Resurrection

One of the most fascinating aspects of the subject of resurrection is this, that the New Testament says more about a general resurrection than it does about the resurrection of Jesus. That Jesus was raised from the dead is considered established fact by the writers of the New Testament, and this is the central tenet of Christian teaching; but more is said about *our* resurrection than Jesus'.

> ***Matthew 22:23-33*** *(Also Mark 12:18 & Luke 20) On that day some Sadducees (**who say there is no resurrection**) came to Jesus and questioned Him, 24 asking, "Teacher, Moses said, 'If a man dies having no children, his brother as next of kin shall marry his wife and raise up children for his brother.' 25 "Now there were seven brothers with us; and the first married and died, and having no children left his wife to his brother; 26 so also the second, and the third, down to the seventh. 27 "Last of all, the woman died. 28 "**In the resurrection**, therefore, whose wife of the seven will she be? For they all had married her."*
>
> *29 But Jesus answered and said to them, "You are mistaken, not understanding the Scriptures nor the power of God. 30 "For **in the resurrection** they neither marry nor are given in marriage, but are like angels in heaven. 31 "But regarding the resurrection of the dead, have you not read what was spoken to you by God: 32 'I am the God of Abraham, and the God of Isaac, and the God of Jacob'? He is not the God of the dead but of the living."*
>
> *33 When the crowds heard this, they were astonished at His teaching.*

The Sadducees, in a mocking debate with Jesus ask Him

questions about a subject they don't believe in: resurrection. The idea was to show Jesus how silly the idea of resurrection is: how could Levirate marriage be carried out in the afterlife? By their understanding, it couldn't work. Jesus' reply is fascinating: He tells them the way it will work. He had no tradition or scripture to work off of; He spoke as one having insider knowledge of how the future will be.

The debate is not over Jesus' resurrection ambitions, but over the basic concept, and Jesus describes what the general resurrection will be like.

> ***Luke 2:34*** *And Simeon blessed them and said to Mary His mother, "Behold, this Child is appointed for the fall and* **rise** *(literally, resurrection) of many in Israel,*

No major translation renders it this way, but the literal Greek says the 'resurrection of many.' This statement is rather enigmatic, perhaps intentionally so, but it can be allowed that Simeon was alluding to Jesus being the initiator of resurrection for the saints.

> ***Luke 14:13-14*** *"But when you give a reception, invite the poor, the crippled, the lame, the blind, 14 and you will be blessed, since they do not have the means to repay you; for you will be repaid* ***at the resurrection*** *of the righteous."*

Here, Jesus is using the general resurrection as an incentive to practice charity to the downtrodden. Our good works will be rewarded, not in This Age, but in The Age to Come. He does not explain or elaborate on what the resurrection is, He simply assumes it will be understood, and says it is a day of reward. This is entirely in keeping with the Biblical concept of the Day of the Lord. Furthermore, it should be noted that Jesus refers to it as the resurrection *of the righteous.*

> ***John 5:28-29*** *"Do not marvel at this; for an hour is coming, in which all who are in the tombs will hear His voice, 29 and will come forth; those who did the good deeds to a resurrection of life, those who committed the evil deeds to a resurrection of judgment.*

This small passage is loaded. First, as we saw earlier, just as Paul says about the DOY, when those who are asleep in Christ will rise, Jesus says they will hear His voice. Second, the resurrection is a double edged sword: there is a resurrection unto life, and a resurrection unto judgment. This is entirely in line with Daniel 12. This also lines up with the concept of the DOY as being a day of deliverance and a day of judgment.

The contrast between the 'two' resurrections is critical: one is unto life, *the other is not.* Judgment is always rendered as being between existence and non-existence. More on this later.

> ***John 11:24-27*** *Martha said to Him, "I know that he will rise again* ***in the resurrection on the last day****." 25 Jesus said to her, "****I am the resurrection*** *and the life; he who believes in Me will live even if he dies, 26 and everyone who lives and believes in Me will never die. Do you believe this?"*

We return to the story of Lazarus being raised from the dead. Previously, we noted that Martha already had a belief in resurrection without knowledge of Jesus' coming experience. Here, we see Jesus saying not that He *will be* resurrected, but that He *is* the *embodiment of the resurrection hope of all people.* Furthermore, He holds out the promise of immortality as rooted in Him, *and only in Him.*

> ***Acts 4:1-2*** *As they were speaking to the people, the priests and the captain of the temple guard and the Sadducees came up to them, 2 being greatly disturbed because they were teaching the people and proclaiming in Jesus* ***the resurrection from the dead.***

It is very important to note what is happening here. The Sadducees are unhappy with the content of the Apostles' teaching. What they are preaching was not about Jesus' resurrection but about the general resurrection which happens *in* Jesus. Just as Paul and Peter link the resurrection of God's people to Jesus' resurrection, we see it here. Those on the Temple grounds listening to Peter and John would not have been shocked by the idea of the resurrection; we have seen that debate was already in play. The new angle is how their resurrection was through the agency of Jesus, who was so recently killed and raised again.

> ***Acts 17:18; 32-34*** *And also some of the Epicurean and Stoic philosophers were conversing with him. Some were saying, "What would this idle babbler wish to say?" Others, "He seems to be a proclaimer of strange deities," —* ***because he was preaching Jesus and the resurrection.***

> ***32-34*** *Now when they heard of the resurrection of the dead, some began to sneer, but others said, "We shall hear you again concerning this." 33 So Paul went out of their midst.*

We have already established that the resurrection of

Jesus was the central topic of Apostolic preaching; but we see that the general resurrection follows closely behind as a main theme. Here in Athens, first in the synagogue, then on Mars Hill, the resurrection becomes the issue of conflict. In both cases, the Greeks are floored by the idea, not because of the miraculous nature of it, but because of the irrelevance of it. This is because of their false premise that the human soul is immortal. Because Paul did not share this presupposition, his main points of theology were hotly debated.

In raising the subject of resurrection at all, Paul was broaching a subject that was completely foreign to Greek thought, as the response shows. Ironically, this exact same reaction is prevalent among Christians today, *because we are more rooted in Greek philosophy that we are in Biblical understanding.*

> ***2 Timothy 2:16-18*** *But avoid worldly and empty chatter, for it will lead to further ungodliness, 17 and their talk will spread like gangrene. Among them are Hymenaeus and Philetus, 18 men who have gone astray from the truth saying that the resurrection has already taken place, and they upset the faith of some.*

This seemingly minor quotation establishes a very important point: resurrection is not yet part of the Christian experience. We know nothing more of Hymenaeus and Philetus; we only know what they taught: that the resurrection has already happened. Paul condemns this thought in his strongest terms. Although not stated clearly, it is apparent that the issue is not the resurrection of Jesus.

The heretics believe in resurrection (unlike those that Paul responds to in 1 Corinthians 15); the problem is that they say the resurrection has already happened *for believers.*

Again, we see that the resurrection is a future event, not a mystical or metaphysical one for the believer in This Age.

> ***Hebrews 6:1-2*** *Therefore leaving the elementary teaching about the Christ, let us press on to maturity, not laying again a foundation of repentance from dead works and of faith toward God, 2 of instruction about washings and laying on of hands, and* ***the resurrection of the dead*** *and eternal judgment.*

We only need to point out that the author of Hebrews here is referring to the coming resurrection of God's people. It is considered an elementary teaching from which the believer should move on to deeper things.

> ***Revelation 20:11-14*** *Then I saw a great white throne and Him who sat upon it, from whose presence earth and heaven fled away, and no place was found for them. 12 And I saw the dead, the great and the small, standing before the throne, and books were opened; and another book was opened, which is the book of life; and the dead were judged from the things which were written in the books, according to their deeds. 13 And the sea gave up the dead which were in it, and death and Hades gave up the dead which were in them; and they were judged, every one of them according to their deeds.*

As Daniel and Jesus spoke of the double edged sword of resurrection, we see it here: all are resurrected, yet they are repeatedly referred to as 'the dead.' They have been raised for judgment, but this is not the life which is the reward of the righteous; it is a passing state for the sole purpose of hearing God's verdict upon us. There is no distinction as to whether the dead are the good or the wicked; it's everybody all at once.

1 Corinthians 15

In writing this letter, Paul was responding to two lines of inquiry. First, Paul had heard rumors about things going on at their church, and wanted to address them (1 Cor. 1:11: "For I have been informed…"). Second, the Corinthians had written to him about some issues and he was responding to their questions (1 Cor. 7:1: "Now concerning the things which you wrote…").

One of the issues that arose apparently was that somebody was denying the doctrine of resurrection in this congregation (1 Cor. 15:12). Some scholars have speculated whether this was part of the original letter by Paul, but in light of the variety of issues which he had already addressed, it is entirely in keeping with the previous 14 chapters, so there's no need to jump to such a conclusion. The entire chapter is devoted to this issue and it is the clearest and most comprehensive statement about resurrection in the Bible. That Paul spent so much time addressing it demonstrates that it was central to his theology. We will tackle the entire passage, section by section.

<u>Vss. 1-2: Introduction: The Foundation of Paul's Teaching</u>

Now I make known to you, brethren, <u>the gospel</u> which I preached to you, which also you received, in which also you stand, 2 <u>by which also you are saved, if you hold fast</u> the word which I preached to you, unless you believed in vain.

Two main points here. <u>First</u>, Paul says that the following is the gospel which he preached. The resurrection is not just a peripheral event which is included *in* the gospel; *it <u>is</u> the gospel!* <u>Second</u>, the first point is underscored by the statement that Paul says we are saved *if we hold to this teaching.* That he makes such a bold declaration is reinforced by how much time he devotes to the subject, in what is the longest chapter of the letter.

<u>Vss. 3-11: The Historic Certainty of Jesus' Resurrection</u>

3 For I delivered to you as of <u>first importance</u> what I also received, that Christ died for our sins according to the Scriptures, 4 and that He was buried, and that <u>He was raised on the third day</u> according to the Scriptures, 5 and that He appeared to Cephas, then to the twelve. 6 After that He appeared to more than five hundred brethren at one time, most of whom remain until now, but <u>some have fallen asleep</u>; 7 then He appeared to James, then to all the apostles; 8 and last of all, as to one untimely born, He appeared to me also. 9 For I am the least of the apostles, and not fit to be called an apostle, because I persecuted the church of God. 10 But by the grace of God

I am what I am, and His grace toward me did not prove vain; but I labored even more than all of them, yet not I, but the grace of God with me. 11 Whether then it was I or they, so we preach and so you believed.

Three points to emphasize: First, Paul says that this teaching is of first importance. Second, that Jesus appeared to over 500 people: Peter, James, the twelve, the apostles (who became apostles by virtue of this appearance), and to Paul himself. Paul does not elaborate when this experience was, but most likely he was referring to the Damascus road encounter. The main point of all this is that Paul insists that the resurrection was an historic event that was observable, not a mystical experience shared by a small handful of devoted followers. Third, once again, 'asleep' is used in reference to the deceased believers.

Vs. 12-19: The Indispensible General Resurrection

12 Now if Christ is preached, that He has been raised from the dead, how do some among you say that there is no resurrection of the dead? 13 But if there is no resurrection of the dead, not even Christ has been raised; 14 and if Christ has not been raised, then our preaching is vain, your faith also is vain. 15 Moreover we are even found to be false witnesses of God, because we testified against God that He raised Christ, whom He did not raise, if in fact the dead are not raised. 16 For if the dead are not raised, not even Christ has been raised; 17 and if Christ has not been raised, your faith is worthless; you are still in your sins. 18 Then those also who have fallen asleep in Christ have perished. 19 If we have hoped in Christ in this life only, we are of all men most to be pitied.

There are five important points for consideration. First, Paul says clearly that Jesus' resurrection is an indispensable piece of the gospel. It is what "has been preached," and this cannot be revoked. Second, notice that in vs. 13, Paul makes the resurrection of Jesus *dependent* upon the doctrine of resurrection. It is logical that Paul would base the teaching of resurrection upon Jesus'; it is unexpected that he would base Jesus' rising upon the doctrine. Just as the resurrection debate was already happening in Israel irrespective of Jesus' ministry, here, it is as though Paul is saying, "See, Jesus proved the Pharisees correct!" (as opposed to the Sadducees).

Third, Paul says in vs. 14, that the resurrection of Jesus is so central, that the Christian faith is a washout if Jesus was not really raised from the dead. Faith is not seen as a noble idea regardless of the facts; it's useless if the facts are not correct. This is so important a point, that he says it again in vs. 17. Fourth, Paul twice in this short section shows in vs. 15 & 16 that *the general resurrection and the Lord's resurrection are interlocking and inseparable.* Neither one is a moot point or a dispensable theological idea. Both are required.

Fifth, and finally, in vs. 18, Paul says that if there is no resurrection, then the deceased have perished. If there was ever a place that the idea of 'dying and going to heaven' were shot down, it's right here. If Paul thought humans possessed an immortal soul, *this* is the place where it would be known. Instead, he says the deceased are already *perished* if Jesus has not been resurrected. If there is some alternative way of existence known to Paul, it would be stated here, but there is none. Immortality is based upon Jesus' resurrection; if He was not raised, then there is no afterlife to speak of. If the resurrection was just one of several options, Paul could list those options here, but he sees none.

Vs. 20-22: Jesus Is the Cause of the Resurrection

20 But now Christ has been raised from the dead, the first fruits of those who are asleep. 21 For since by a man came death, ***by a man also came the resurrection*** *of the dead. 22 For as in Adam all die, so also in Christ all will be made alive.*

Two points to draw out here. First, Paul uses the Jewish feast of First Fruits as a type to explain the resurrection. Based upon Exodus 23:16, the Feast of First Fruits was a mandated act of worship for ancient Israel. The idea was that some of the harvest has matured and that the remainder will soon mature as well. Rather than wait to see if it would be a good year for the produce, they were to assume it would be and worship in faith right then and there rather than waiting to see if there would be more crops. Using this, Paul says Jesus was the 'first fruits' of the resurrection 'harvest'; there would be more to come, meaning His followers.

Second, Paul says that the general resurrection (which most of his Jewish contemporaries believed in), was dependent upon Jesus. The Messiah is the reason that there will be a resurrection. This is the reverse of the previous section, where Paul considers the resurrection of Jesus to be dependent upon a general resurrection. Here, he says the general resurrection is dependent upon Jesus. Again, the two are interlocking and inseparable. This echoes exactly Jesus' statement that "I AM the resurrection" (John 11:25).

Vs. 23-28: The Order of the General Resurrection Event

23 But each ***in his own order: Christ the first fruits, after that*** *those who are Christ's at His coming, 24* ***then comes the end****, when He hands over the kingdom to the God and Father, when He has* ***abolished all rule and all authority and power****. 25 For He must reign until He has put all His enemies under His feet. 26* ***The last enemy that will be abolished is death****. 27 For HE HAS PUT ALL THINGS IN SUBJECTION UNDER HIS FEET. But when He says, "All things are put in subjection," it is evident that He is excepted who put all things in subjection to Him. 28 When all things are subjected to Him, then the Son Himself also will be subjected to the One who subjected all things to Him, so that God may be all in all.*

There are four main points to consider here. First, Paul hints at a similar order of events as found in 1 Thessalonians 4:15-16: *For this we say to you by the word of the Lord, that* ***we who are alive*** *and remain until the coming of the Lord,* ***will not precede those who have fallen asleep***. Second, the unfolding of the Day of Yahweh/Christ Jesus is this: Jesus returns, the dead are raised, the living are joined with them, and then comes the end and judgment. Third, the 'cosmic hierarchy' known as powers and principalities (Rom. 8:38, Eph. 6:12, Heb. 6:5 & 1 Peter 3:22) will be dealt with.

Fourth, death is the last trace of evil to be eliminated. This timeline of events presented here is consistent with other passages, most notably Rev. 20. There is resurrection, judgment, the destruction of evil and then the reward of life for those in Christ. The conclusion of Isaiah promised the end of death; Jesus said He had overcome death, and Paul echoes this thought here. Death was the great evil which God warned us about in the Garden of Eden and which the serpent covered up with a lie.

Vs. 29-34: Resurrection and Conduct

29 Otherwise, what will those do who are baptized for the dead? ***If the dead are not raised at all****, why then are they baptized for them? 30 Why are we also in danger every hour? 31 I affirm, brethren, by the boasting in you which I have in Christ Jesus our Lord, I die daily. 32 If from human motives I fought with wild beasts at Ephesus, what does it profit me? If the dead are not raised, 'let us eat and drink, for tomorrow we die.' 33 Do not be deceived: "Bad company corrupts good morals." 34 Become sober-minded as you ought, and stop sinning; for some have no knowledge of God. I speak this to your shame.*

There are three points to emphasize here. First, Paul again bases his argument upon the general resurrection. Baptism for the dead is an issue which has puzzled scholars since the earliest days, and we won't unravel it here; however, the point remains that the reason for it in Paul's mind was the resurrection. Second, Paul's entire life of suffering for the cause is because of the resurrection. His whole ministry came down to believing in this one doctrine above all others; otherwise, he wouldn't bother with the hardships. Third, Paul again indicates that if there is no resurrection, then it's all over when we die and there is no future to speak of. Again, Paul couldn't possibly believe that people 'die and go to heaven' and make this statement. Any post death existence is rooted only in the belief in a future resurrection.

Vs. 35-50: Resurrection Bodies

35 But someone will say, "How are the dead raised? ***And***
with what kind of body do they come?" *36 You fool! That*
which you sow does not come to life unless it dies; 37 and that
which you sow, ***you do not sow the body which is to be****, but*
a bare grain, perhaps of wheat or of something else. 38 But God
gives it a body just as He wished, and to each of the seeds a body
of its own. 39 ***All flesh is not the same flesh****, but there is*
one flesh of men, and another flesh of beasts, and another flesh of
birds, and another of fish. 40 There are also heavenly bodies and
earthly bodies, but the glory of the heavenly is one, and the glory
of the earthly is another. 41 There is one glory of the sun, and
another glory of the moon, and another glory of the stars; for star
differs from star in glory.

42 So also is the resurrection of the dead. ***It is sown a***
perishable body, it is raised an imperishable body;

43 it is sown in dishonor, it is raised in glory; it is sown in weak-
ness, it is raised in power; 44 it is sown a natural body, it is
raised a spiritual body. If there is a natural body, there is also a
spiritual body. 45 So also it is written, "The first MAN, Adam,
BECAME A LIVING SOUL." The last Adam became a
life-giving spirit. 46 However, the spiritual is not first, but the
natural; then the spiritual. 47 The first man is from the earth,
earthy (literally in Greek: made of dust. Author's note)*;*
the second man is from heaven. 48 As is the earthy, so also are
those who are earthy; and as is the heavenly, so also are those who
are heavenly. 49 Just as we have borne the image of the earthy,
we will also bear the image of the heavenly. 50 Now I say this,
brethren, ***that flesh and blood cannot inherit the king-***
dom of God; *nor does the perishable inherit the imperishable.*

Because Paul repeatedly uses the word 'body', many mistakenly believe that he is teaching a type of dualism where the soul is separated from the physical body, but Paul never teaches anything of the sort. Whenever he speaks of the body, he is assuming that the "inner person" is bound up with it. He is not speaking about a mortal body which has been paired up with an immortal soul; we've established that the Biblical belief is that humans are completely and thoroughly mortal in all aspects.

Having said that, there are two main points to make here. First, Paul declares that the body that comes in the resurrection is a completely different type of body, just as fish and birds have different bodies than humans. The analogy is that these bodies are adapted to specific purposes and environments. Likewise, the resurrection body will be one that is suited for eternal glory. Second, unlike our current bodies, the resurrection body will be immortal. In vs. 50, Paul says that it is impossible for us to receive the full weight of the Kingdom of God with our current 'equipment'. He does not elaborate on why this is so.

Vs. 51-58: The Resurrection Moment

51 Behold, I tell you a mystery; ***we will not all sleep, but we will all be changed****, 52 in a moment, in the twinkling of an eye, at the last trumpet; for the trumpet will sound,* ***and the dead will be raised imperishable, and we will be changed.*** *53* ***For this perishable must put on the imperishable****, and* ***this mortal must put on immortality****. 54 But when this perishable will have put on the imperishable, and this mortal will have put on immortality, Then will come about the saying that is written: "Death is swallowed up in victory. 55 "O death where is your victory? O death, where is your sting?" 56 The sting of death is sin, and the power of sin is the law; 57 but thanks be to God, who gives us the victory through our Lord Jesus Christ. 58 Therefore, my beloved brethren, be steadfast, immovable, always abounding in the work of the Lord, knowing that your toil is not in vain in the Lord.*

Paul wraps up his teaching on resurrection with this, that it will happen instantaneously, just as Jesus said His return would be like lightning flashing from one end of the sky to the other. Besides this, Paul has made these points previously. Some will be dead, and some will be alive when the Day of the Lord comes. The dead will be resurrected. The living and the dead will be changed into a new kind of physicality, and the new physicality will be immortal, unlike the previous. Again, it is mistaken to read this as a dualism separating the soul from the physical body.

In discussions upon the subject of resurrection, the point I hear repeatedly is the belief that when the resurrection occurs, that this is when the soul is rejoined with the body. This point is seriously faulty; for the simple fact is that the Bible *nowhere* says that this is what happens. It is inferred because people start with the falsehood that we possess immortal souls. The Bible nowhere says this, either.

I cannot emphasize this enough, so I will lay it out again.

A) The Bible nowhere speaks of an immortal soul.

B) The Bible nowhere says the soul separates from the body, either to heaven or hell.

C) The Bible nowhere says that souls will be rejoined to bodies at a future point in the resurrection or otherwise.

THEREFORE, the general resurrection is about the total and utter remaking of a person for a life that lasts for eternity. Paul had no other spiritual or metaphysical option for humanity: if there was no resurrection of Jesus, and if there is no general resurrection, then there is no hope for overcoming death. Not a metaphorical or allegorical death, but true, final, bitter, total death.

SUMMARY

Resurrection could be said to be the point of the whole gospel. Death reigns, and Jesus came to overturn death. He died, was resurrected, and His resurrection becomes the source of all future resurrection. Having a firm handle on this idea is not a peripheral tangent of Christianity; it is the main point. Having said that, what do we see?

First, the Old Testament gave some indicators of resurrection, but they are rare and obscure. Sometimes, resurrection is a metaphor for the revival of the nation of Israel. However, there are also times when resurrection clearly indicates the bringing back to life of the individual.

Second, in Isaiah and Daniel, resurrection is held out only for the righteous. Daniel says that some are resurrected unto disgrace and everlasting contempt, and the righteous unto life. Isaiah echoes this by saying the wicked will be mere corpses for the righteous to look upon.

Third, resurrection evidently went through theological development in between the Old and New Testaments. Apart from Jesus, the Sadducees and Pharisees in the gospels already have a defined debate over the concept, with the Sadducees rejecting the idea and the Pharisees embracing it. In Martha, we see a layperson who was versed in the belief.

Fourth, we see that the idea of resurrection was not easily accepted across the board by "pre-scientific, ignorant primitives." Repeatedly, we see a hostile reaction to the concept. For those today who would assume that people back then readily believed in this sort of thing, we find them to be wrong. The apostles made the resurrection the centerpoint of their teaching *even though it caused repeated rejection.* If resurrection was a manufactured event to 'sell' a new religion, it certainly didn't work. Yet, the apostles retained the belief *because they believed it to be true.*

Fifth, although we did not examine the gospel passages involved, they do make a clear point that the resurrection of Jesus was very much a physical experience and not a mystical or metaphorical one. Resurrection was not a code word for a 'spiritual' happening that was unobservable, but an experience that was empirical in nature. If Christianity was a manufactured religion, the early church could have made it much easier to promote if they settled for a 'spiritualized' concept, but they didn't. They hung on to the idea of a physical resurrection despite opposition.

Sixth, that Jesus experienced a physical resurrection is strongly supported by the fact that there seems to be no debate that the tomb was empty. Believers and enemies alike seem to agree on this point. *The argument was over what happened to the body.* The authorities in Jerusalem certainly didn't steal it, otherwise they could have produced the corpse and stopped the Christian movement in its infancy. This leaves only two options. A) Either the disciples stole the body and then promoted a myth, or B) Jesus did truly rise from the dead. Obviously, my point of view is that

Jesus did truly rise from the dead; but there can be no doubt at all that the tomb was empty.

Seventh, for all our discussion about Jesus rising from the dead, it is important to remember that more is said about the resurrection of God's people in the New Testament than about Jesus'. In 1 Corinthians 15, Paul makes the two ideas inseparable and interlocking as though to say we can't have one without the other.

Eighth, for those who would transform the resurrection into some mystical spiritual experience that is already experienced by believers, we see in 2 Timothy that Paul clearly condemns this idea. Resurrection is a future experience, although some people in the Biblical history were raised from the dead.

Ninth, while people were raised or resuscitated from the dead in Scripture, the true ultimate resurrection is an event at the end of history. Paul makes it clear that the true resurrection results in everlasting life; anybody raised from the dead in the past ultimately died again.

Tenth, Rev. 20 uses the 'Daniel formula' of all people being resurrected for the purpose of judgment. The dead are all raised and gathered to one place for the verdict. The implication of this is that there is a consistent timeline given in scripture: death > resurrection > judgment > reward/punishment. This leaves no room for the idea of dying and then going to heaven or hell.

Eleventh, the resurrection comes with a new kind of body. What kind of body is resurrected? We are not told. What we are told is that whatever we 'arrive' with, it becomes something else for the present 'equipment' is inadequate for what we will inherit.

Twelfth, as we saw previously, the resurrection happens with the return of Jesus on the Day of the Lord. We are not resurrected at different times, but all together at once. Resurrection is not a different way to say "die and go to heaven" but a specific event that awaits us in the future.

A CONFLICT? RESURRECTION & TRANSFORMATION

Because of the way he phrases things, the apostle Paul can be misunderstood. He lays out a clear timeline of resurrection and new life, but he seems to say it in different ways. He says in Philippians 3:21 that Jesus will transform our bodies. He says this in 1 Corinthians 15 as well. However, in the latter, Paul says the dead shall be raised imperishable, and the living will be transformed, with no mention of judgment or subsequent events. Is Paul inconsistent? I think not. I believe what we see here is Paul writing an abbreviated account of what he says elsewhere.

As an example you might see me getting into my car with some luggage, and so you ask, "Where are you going?" I could reply "To the airport" or "To Chicago" or "To Europe". In fact I could be asked this by three separate people and give each a different answer. Does this mean I'm telling any of them a falsehood? Not at all. If I am driving to the airport to fly to Chicago where I will catch another plane to London, then I can tell anyone who asks just one part of the story. This does not mean my story is changing.

I could tell one person that I am going to London, which implies going to the airport. It also might require a previous destination such as Chicago, or it might be a direct flight. If I say "the airport" the implication is that I am flying somewhere. Or, it could be that I am only delivering a bag there for somebody else. If I say I'm going to London, then the steps in between are all assumed.

What Paul is doing in 1 Corinthians is giving the summed up result of resurrection. Jesus will return (like a flash of lightning, or in the twinkling of an eye), raise the dead, gather the living, and together we will face judgment. Afterwards, those in Christ will be transformed into glorious existence. In speaking as he does, Paul is assuming the in-between steps and saying that "we will be transformed." This is not a contradiction in theology.

Part Two Summary

We saw in Part Two that the various streams of ideas intertwined and were almost impossible to keep separate. Indeed, they are overlapping and interlocking. Because each chapter has so much detail, it will be useful to "sum up the summaries" so that we have a unified, singular picture of what scripture teaches.

First, the Day of the Lord, or Day of Yahweh (DOY) was depicted in the Old Testament as the ultimate mega event. Sometimes the term is used as judgment within history, but it also is used to end history.

Second, the DOY has two edges to it. On the one hand, it is a day of destruction for the wicked. On the other hand, it is a day of deliverance for God's people. The prophet Amos mixes the two notions by warning the Israelites that being descended from Abraham is not a guarantee of deliverance for them against the gentiles. Instead, it is fraught with dangers for them, too.

Third, we see in the New Testament that the DOY is not dropped as a relic of "Old Testament thinking" but is still very central to early church. The change comes in that it becomes the "Day of Jesus Christ". Jesus makes reference to "His day", and Paul outright equates Jesus with Yahweh by his reference to "the day of the Lord Jesus." This is no slight tweaking of wording, but a major theological declaration.

Fourth, in his first letter to the Thessalonians, Paul utilizes the double sided nature of the DOY, saying it will come like a thief in the night, and that destruction will come upon the wicked. In the same passage, he states that believers should not be caught off guard by the DOY, and furthermore, we will be spared the wrath of God, which has always been associated with the DOY. In 2 Thess. 2, Paul says the DOY will not come until the apostasy comes first.

Fifth, we see the signal of the DOY by the term "on that day". Jesus equates "that day" with His return and with judgment.

Sixth, in speaking about the return of Jesus, it is clear that it is a final, decisive event, not a secret or quietly progressing one. Jesus said it will be like a flood or a flash of lightning. Repeatedly, Jesus refers to the aspect of final judgment with His return.

Seventh, Where the Old Testament hinted at resurrection, the New Testament greatly expands the concept. Jesus was resurrected in bodily form, and Paul says we shall enjoy the same experience that Jesus had. Paul says that we will receive the kind of body the Jesus had upon resurrection, and this body will be one built to last eternity. Then, Paul ties the general resurrection to the return of Jesus, which is on the DOY, which is now the DOJC. In fact, in one passage (1 Thess. 4:13-5:3) Paul clearly ties together the return of Jesus, the resurrection and the DOY. By implication, judgment is included.

Eighth, just as the book of Revelation does, Paul states that the return of Jesus will be preceded by an agent of Satan who will perform false signs and wonders. This ties into Jesus' warning to not follow anybody claiming to be Him, because His return will be instantaneous, quick, decisive and final. True believers will not have to ponder whether somebody is Jesus, for they know if Jesus comes there will be no time to think about it. If you're wondering if somebody is actually Jesus, *he isn't.*

Ninth, the implications of this approach are profound. If we follow the truly Biblical framework presented through both the Old and New Testament, then we realize that all talk of rapture, tribulation and millennium is unnecessary and superfluous. Yes, there will tribulations, false messiahs and the return of Jesus, but His return is the end of history, the Day of Yahweh. The DOY punctuates history and ends it.

Part Three: The Age to Come

In this section, we see how many of the threats and promises carried by both the Old and New Testament are fulfilled. Repeatedly, the Old Testament says in one manner or another the wicked will be cut off or destroyed. There are also promises of unimaginable glory for God's people. In both cases, these are fulfilled at the end point in history.

The Day of Yahweh/Jesus Christ is the agent which brings these predictions to completion and thus ushers in The Age to Come.

9. Destruction of the Wicked (Old Testament)
10. Destruction of the Wicked (New Testament).
11. The New Jerusalem
12. The Tree of Life

9

Destruction of the Wicked (Old Testament)

From the very beginning of the Bible, one choice is consistently presented to humanity, and that is the choice between life and death. In the Garden of Eden, God warned that disobedience would result in death, and the serpent contradicted Him and said it wouldn't. Moses said to the Israelites, "Choose life" by obeying the Lord's commands (Deut. 30:19). The most famous verse of the New Testament, John 3:16, presents a choice between life and perishing.

In western Christianity, we have learned to read Scripture through the lens of Greek thought, which mostly held to a belief in the immortal soul. Because we have this presupposition, we do not take Scripture at its face value. But if you can put aside that bias, you can see that the Bible is actually teaching a sobering truth: *the wicked will be destroyed.* As we will see, the Old Testament is perfectly clear on this point.

With that in mind, let us look at a few quick examples and they we will make some observations about them.

Psalm 1

How blessed is the man who does not walk in the counsel of the wicked,

Nor stand in the path of sinners, nor sit in the seat of scoffers!

2 But his delight is in the law of the LORD, and in His law he meditates day and night.

3 He will be like a tree firmly planted by streams of water,

Which yields its fruit in its season and its leaf does not wither;

And in whatever he does, he prospers.

4 The wicked are not so, but they are like chaff which the wind drives away.

5 Therefore the wicked will not stand in the judgment,

Nor sinners in the assembly of the righteous.

6 For the LORD knows the way of the righteous, but the way of the wicked will perish.

Psalm 37:7-11

7 Rest in the LORD and wait patiently for Him;

Do not fret because of him who prospers in his way,

Because of the man who carries out wicked schemes.

8 Cease from anger and forsake wrath; do not fret, it leads only to evildoing.

9 For evildoers will be cut off, but those who wait for the LORD, they will inherit the land.

10 Yet a little while and the wicked man will be no more;

And you will look carefully for his place and he will not be there.

11 But the humble will inherit the land

And will delight themselves in abundant prosperity.

Isaiah 66:22-24

22 "For just as the new heavens and the new earth

Which I make will endure before Me," declares the LORD,

"So your offspring and your name will endure.

23 "And it shall be from new moon to new moon And from sabbath to sabbath,

All mankind will come to bow down before Me," says the LORD.

24 "Then they will go forth and look on the corpses of the men who have transgressed against Me.

For their worm will not die, and their fire will not be quenched; and they will be an abhorrence to all mankind."

Here are three points which should be obvious. First, in Psalm 1, there is a clear reference to judgment day, with the implication that the wicked will be destroyed ("will not stand"). Second, in each passage, the point is unmistakable: the wicked will cease to be. Their fate is not an unhappy existence, or a less than satisfying existence; it is *non-existence.* Terms like "cut off" and "corpses' are clear references to a deceased condition. Third, and most importantly, this fate is not in the here and now, but is a verdict to be decided *at the end of time.* Judgment day is referred to in Psalm 1; Isaiah hints at this destruction as being an end time event.

Some will read verses like these and conclude that they promise prosperity in the here and now for the faithful, but the contexts and contents clearly show that they point to an ultimate, final result. As one person once said to me, "Psalms and Proverbs teach that the righteous will prosper, and the Ecclesiastes follows and says 'But not necessarily'". This understanding comes from not seeing what is actually being pointed to. Generally speaking, it is a true principle that in the here and now God is inclined to prosper His people; but the deeper truth that is being conveyed in these passages is that the Day of Yahweh / Jesus Christ will fulfill these promises of prosperity and justice.

Having used these three passages as the template, it is time to demonstrate how pervasive this teaching is throughout the Old Testament. Previously, we've established that the Bible nowhere teaches of an immortal soul; therefore, we must eliminate that presupposition. Having done so, let us read the following passages:

Psalm 21:7-11

7 For the king trusts in the LORD,

And through the lovingkindness of the Most High he will not be shaken.

8 Your hand will find out all your enemies;

Your right hand will find out those who hate you.

9 You will make them as a fiery oven in the time of your anger;

The LORD will swallow them up in His wrath, and fire will devour them.

10 Their offspring You will destroy from the earth,

And their descendants from among the sons of men.

11 Though they intended evil against You and devised a plot, They will not succeed.

Psalm 50:22-23

22 "Now consider this, you who forget God,

Or I will tear you in pieces, and there will be none to deliver.

23 "He who offers a sacrifice of thanksgiving honors Me;

And to him who orders his way aright I shall show the salvation of God."

Surely there is a God who judges on earth!"

Psalm 58:10-11

10 The righteous will rejoice when he sees the vengeance;

He will wash his feet in the blood of the wicked.

11 And men will say, "Surely there is a reward for the righteous;

Isaiah 1:27-31

27 Zion will be redeemed with justice And her repentant ones with righteousness.

28 But transgressors and sinners will be crushed together,

And those who forsake the LORD will come to an end.

29 Surely you will be ashamed of the oaks which you have desired,

And you will be embarrassed at the gardens which you have chosen.

30 For you will be like an oak whose leaf fades away

Or as a garden that has no water.

31 The strong man will become tinder, His work also a spark.

Thus they shall both burn together And there will be none to quench them.

Isaiah 11:4-5

4 But with righteousness He will judge the poor,
And decide with fairness for the afflicted of the earth;
And He will strike the earth with the rod of His mouth,
And with the breath of His lips He will slay the wicked.
5 Also righteousness will be the belt about His loins,
And faithfulness the belt about His waist.

Isaiah 51:7-8

7 "Listen to Me, you who know righteousness, A people in whose heart is My law;

Do not fear the reproach of man, nor be dismayed at their revilings.

8 "For the moth will eat them like a garment, and the grub will eat them like wool.

But My righteousness will be forever, and My salvation to all generations."

There will be many who say that these speak of immediate judgment within history, but the case does not hold up. Over and over again, we see that in life, the wicked keep getting ahead. This point of view nowhere better seen than in Psalm 73:

> ***Psalm 73:15-20***
>
> *15 If I had said, "I will speak thus,"*
>
> *Behold, I would have betrayed the generation of Your children.*
>
> *16 When I pondered to understand this, It was troublesome in my sight*
>
> *17 Until I came into the sanctuary of God; Then I perceived their end.*
>
> *18 Surely You set them in slippery places; You cast them down to destruction.*
>
> *19 How they are destroyed in a moment!*
>
> *They are utterly swept away by sudden terrors!*
>
> *20 Like a dream when one awakes, O Lord, when aroused, You will despise their form.*

The previous verses in this lament speaks of how the righteous get crushed and how the wicked prosper. The attitude of the Psalmist changes when he considers the end of time in judgment day. It absolutely refers to two things: A) a future verdict, and B) the resulting destruction, and it cannot be interpreted any other way.

The Special Evidence of Ezekiel 18

This chapter is particularly conclusive. The main point of the 32 verses within it is simple: people will be punished for their own sins, not for the sins of their parents. There are two refrains which repeatedly occur: "He shall live" and "He shall die." We'll look at a sample from this chapter:

> **Ezekiel 18:5-13** *5 "But if a man is righteous and practices justice and righteousness, 6 and does not eat at the mountain shrines or lift up his eyes to the idols of the house of Israel, or defile his neighbor's wife or approach a woman during her menstrual period — 7 if a man does not oppress anyone, but restores to the debtor his pledge, does not commit robbery, but gives his bread to the hungry and covers the naked with clothing, 8 if he does not lend money on interest or take increase, if he keeps his hand from iniquity and executes true justice between man and man, 9 if he walks in My statutes and My ordinances so as to deal faithfully — he is righteous and will surely live," declares the Lord GOD.*
>
> *10 "Then he may have a violent son who sheds blood and who does any of these things to a brother 11(though he himself did not do any of these things), that is, he even eats at the mountain shrines, and defiles his neighbor's wife, 12 oppresses the poor and needy, commits robbery, does not restore a pledge, but lifts up his eyes to the idols and commits abomination, 13 he lends money on interest and takes increase; will he live? He will not live! He has committed all these abominations, he will surely be put to death; his blood will be on his own head."*

When the whole chapter is read, one point becomes undeniable: the verdict of death or life cannot be rendered within this life, *but only after this life!* The time is allowed for repentance, but there is also time for the righteous to stray from the path of life (vs. 24). This whole chapter only works if viewed as referring to after life *in This Age.* Otherwise, the meaning would be that when the righteous turned to wickedness, he would die on the spot. It can't work. The closing admonition in verse 32 is this: *"For I have no pleasure in the death of anyone who dies," declares the Lord GOD. "Therefore, repent and live."* Again, this cannot refer to life and death in the here & now; it can only refer to the after life.

The Day of Yahweh

Having already covered the Day of the Lord in part two, there is no need to revisit all the passages we discussed there. However, it does serve our purpose to point out that in each of those Old Testament passages, the looming threat was one of *destruction.* Add all of those passages to the list above, and it becomes unmistakable: the Old Testament warns that the wicked will be destroyed.

10

Destruction of the Wicked (New Testament)

As we saw in the previous chapter, the Old Testament repeatedly forewarned that the wicked would be destroyed. The vital point of the passages we examined is that this destruction takes place not in This Age, but in The Age to Come, after the Day of Yahweh. Having established that, the question surfaces: does this fact contradict the New Testament teaching? After all, if we believe in inspired Scripture, then both the Old and New Testaments should teach the same basic things.

Having said that, the point of this chapter is that there is no conflict, that the entire Biblical witness points to the destruction of the wicked, and not just the Old Testament. This may seem like an innovation, but the truth is that the weight of the New Testament is behind the destruction of the wicked; the problem is that people have been taught *not* to see it.

There are four main components that we will examine: Gehenna, Weeping & Gnashing of Teeth, Perishing, and the Lake of Fire.

GEHENNA

Gehenna is the Greek transliteration of the Hebrew word Hinnom. This was an actual place, just outside the walls of Jerusalem. It was where Solomon practiced human sacrifice to the god Molech (1 Kings 11:7). Because of it's repeated misuse for idolatry in Jewish history, it was considered defiled and so by the time of the New Testament, it had become a garbage dump, and such it was in Jesus' day. It was a smelly, smoldering heap of debris, always burning in order to dispose of waste.

It is very important to note that Gehenna is *not* the same as Sheol or Hades. We've discussed those two locales already, and the most important difference is that they are not described as places of punishment, whereas Gehenna is.

There are 12 instances of the word Gehenna in the New Testament, and it is always translated "Hell." Thus, the garbage dump of Jesus' day became a metaphor for judgment on the wicked. Not all the passages describe the nature of Gehenna, but here are the pertinent examples.

> ***Matthew 10:28*** *"Do not fear those who kill the body but are unable to kill the soul; but rather fear Him who is able to destroy both soul and body in hell [Gehenna]."*

There is an important truth in this exhortation from

Jesus. He tells His disciples to stay faithful, even to death. His admonition has weight only because He says that God can *destroy* people entirely, but mortals can only kill the body. To be killed by another person is to cease existence in the here and now; the parallel is that God can end the existence of an individual in the future.

> ***Matthew 18:8, 9*** *"If your hand or your foot causes you to stumble, cut it off and throw it from you; it is better for you to enter life crippled or lame, than to have two hands or two feet and be cast into the* ***eternal fire****. If your eye causes you to stumble, pluck it out and throw it from you. It is better for you to enter life with one eye, than to have two eyes and be cast into the* ***fiery hell [Gehenna]****."*

Again, Jesus' admonition depends upon the threat of destruction. It is not as clear as our previous passage, but notice how the warning works. Jesus is saying that it is better to destroy only part of yourself now, than to be destroyed entirely in Gehenna. Note also that the alternative to Gehenna is *life*. Gehenna is fiery, which is the dominant characteristic of judgment throughout the Old Testament. (Another interpretation is that this applies to judgment upon Jerusalem in its overthrow by the Romans in 70AD).

Listed below are the other verses that refer to Gehenna/ Hell.

> ***Matthew 5:22*** *"But I say to you that everyone who is angry with his brother shall be guilty before the court; and whoever says to his brother, 'You good-for-nothing,' shall be guilty before the*

supreme court; and whoever says, 'You fool,' shall be guilty enough to go into the ***fiery hell.***"

Matthew 5:29, 30 *"If your right eye makes you stumble, tear it out and throw it from you; for it is better for you to lose one of the parts of your body, than for your whole body to be thrown into* ***hell.*** *30 " If your right hand makes you stumble, cut it off and throw it from you; for it is better for you to lose one of the parts of your body, than for your whole body to go into* ***hell.***"

Matthew 23:15 *"Woe to you, scribes and Pharisees, hypocrites, because you travel around on sea and land to make one proselyte; and when he becomes one, you make him twice as much a son of* ***hell*** *as yourselves."*

Matthew 23:33 *"You serpents, you brood of vipers, how will you escape the sentence of* ***hell?***"

Mark 9:43 *If your hand causes you to stumble, cut it off; it is better for you to enter life crippled, than, having your two hands, to go into* ***hell****, into the unquenchable fire…"*

Mark 9:45 *"If your foot causes you to stumble, cut it off; it is better for you to enter life lame, than, having your two feet, to be cast into* ***hell****…"*

Mark 9:47 *"If your eye causes you to stumble, throw it out; it is better for you to enter the kingdom of God with one eye, than, having two eyes, to be cast into* ***hell****…"*

Luke 12:5 *"But I will warn you whom to fear: fear the One who, after He has killed, has authority to cast into* ***hell;*** *yes, I tell you, fear Him!"*

James 3:6 *And the tongue is a fire, the very world of iniquity; the tongue is set among our members asthat which defies* *the entire body, and sets on fire the course of our life, and is set on fire by* ***hell.***

The verses above do not expand our understanding, but they do point out two important features. First, Gehenna is the place of judgment and punishment, and second, that the motif of fire is consistent. Were we not taught to misinterpret these passages, the logical and clearest understanding would be that Gehenna is a place of destruction. We've incorporated the idea of everlasting punishment *into* these verses, but within the verses themselves, another idea is taught. Some might point out the word "eternal" as indicating everlasting punishment, but we will return to that later in this chapter.

WEEPING AND GNASHING OF TEETH

In the following passages, Jesus is talking about the utter, heartbreaking remorse that the wicked will endure in the afterlife. Weeping and gnashing of teeth is not something afflicted upon them from without, but their response to the judgment which has been handed them. It obviously indicates conscious regret by the individual.

Matthew8:11,12(Parallel:Luke13:26) *"Isaytoyou that many will come from east and west, and recline at the table with Abraham, Isaac and Jacob in the kingdom of heaven; but the sons of the kingdom will be cast out into the outer darkness; in that place there will be weeping and gnashing of teeth."*

We see here an interesting aspect of the judgment

verdict. Sometimes, the place in question (which is not named), is the outer darkness, as it is here. Other times it is a place of fire, which fits what we've learned about Gehenna. In this passage, Jesus is warning His Jewish audience that they will be cast away from God while Gentiles are brought near to share in the blessings of the kingdom. The response of those who are cast away will be deep utter anguish, a conscious reaction to the verdict.

> ***Matthew 13:41, 42*** *"The Son of Man will send forth His angels, and they will gather out of His kingdom all stumbling blocks, and those who commit lawlessness, and will throw them into the furnace of fire; in that place there will be weeping and gnashing of teeth.*

The context of these verses is Jesus' discussion of the end of the age, as related in the parable of the wheat and tares. The point of the parable is that the Kingdom of God will co-exist for a time with the kingdom of darkness. At the end of the age, then the good and wicked will be separated and the wicked cast into destruction. In this case the weeping and gnashing of teeth seems to be not only deep regret, but possibly pain. The anguish is unbearable to those who are condemned.

> ***Matthew 13:49, 50*** *"So it will be at the end of the age; the angels will come forth and take out the wicked from among the righteous, and will throw them into the furnace of fire; in that place there will be weeping and gnashing of teeth.*

This is a reiteration by Jesus of the point made previously, as He further explains the parable of the wheat and tares.

Matthew 24:50-51 *. . . The master of that slave will come on a day when he does not expect him and at an hour which he does not know, and will cut him in pieces and assign him a place with the hypocrites; in that place there will be weeping and gnashing of teeth.*

These verses are a mother lode for our understanding as taught in this study. First, notice the judgment is concurrent with the return of Jesus, as taught in The Day of Jesus Christ. Second, notice how the time of His return is unknown and unexpected for non-believers, just as Jesus and Paul taught. Third, notice that instead of fire or darkness as the motif of judgment, it is dismemberment (as in Psalm 50:22). Just as fire is ultimately fatal, so is being hacked to pieces. Both serve as metaphors for the destruction of the wicked.

Matthew 25:29, 30 *"For to everyone who has, more shall be given, and he will have an abundance; but from the one who does not have, even what he does have shall be taken away. 30 "Throw out the worthless slave into the outer darkness; in that place there will be weeping and gnashing of teeth.*

In this conclusion of the parable of the Talents, Jesus again uses the outer darkness as a place of bitterly emotional, and possibly physical torment. The verdict is hinged upon the return of the master (vs. 27), which again fits the idea that the Day of Yahweh/Jesus Christ is the day of Jesus' return.

In concluding this subject, an important and reasonable question is this: doesn't the fact that the wicked will 'weep and gnash their teeth' demonstrate everlasting conscious punishment? The answer is, "No, it doesn't." It demonstrates *conscious* punishment, *but not an everlasting one.* The point of judgment is for God to show the wicked their folly in being unrepentant. The destruction of the wicked will be something the victims will perceive to be taking place, and the suffering will be horrific; but we cannot and should not assume it will be everlasting.

PERISHING

One of the great enigmas of Christian theology to me is how a word that so plainly means one thing can be interpreted to mean the exact opposite. Both of the words "destroy" and "perish" become metaphors for "living unhappily forever." If the writers of scripture wanted to convey an eternity of conscious suffering, they had other words at their disposal; why would they use words that could so easily mean something else and risk being misunderstood?

I believe the main reason that 'destruction' and 'perishing' came to mean the opposite is because Christian teachers long ago ran with an unbiblical presupposition: the immortality of the soul. As we've established already, the Bible nowhere says that the soul is immortal, therefore the logical conclusion in light of this is to take words like 'destruction' and 'perishing' literally.

Some try to get around this by saying that something can continue to exist but cease to function. For example, you can 'destroy' the engine of a car by not putting oil into it. The engine will freeze up and no longer turn over so as to propel the car, and it will continue to exist, but without ability to fully function. In the same manner, a person who is 'destroyed' by Gehenna will cease to 'function' properly, but continue to exist.

This is a logical argument, but I don't think it is a Biblical one. The opposite of God's condemnation is always rendered as 'Life'. If the Bible in its entirety wanted to convey existing forever in torment, there were better ways to phrase it. Instead of a choice between "life" and "perishing", we would have in its place, "everlasting bliss" and "everlasting sorrow." This choice is *never* presented; it is *always* a choice between life and death.

The Greek word for 'perishing' is *apollumi.* Sometimes it means to die, sometimes it's used to indicate 'lost.' When the disciples were in the boat in the storm, this is the word they used to indicate that they were going to die by drowning. *Apollumi* was the Greek word used to translate the Hebrew word for 'destroy' in the Old Testament, and almost always meant utter destruction of a place or a person.

With that in mind, let us look at the following verses.

> ***Matthew 26:52*** *Then Jesus said to him, "Put your sword back into its place; for all those who take up the sword shall* ***perish*** *by the sword.*

The meaning here is plain, as Jesus is speaking literally. He rebukes Peter because he resorted to violence to defend Jesus against His captors. The meaning of 'perish' is quite literal, although it is not in reference to the afterlife.

> ***Luke 13:1-5*** *Now on the same occasion there were some present who reported to Him about the Galileans whose blood Pilate had mixed with their sacrifices. 2 And Jesus said to them, "Do you suppose that these Galileans were greater sinners than all other Galileans because they suffered this fate? 3 "I tell you, no, but unless you repent, you will all likewise* ***perish****. 4 "Or do you suppose that those eighteen on whom the tower in Siloam fell and killed them were worse culprits than all the men who live in Jerusalem? 5 "I tell you, no, but unless you repent, you will all likewise* ***perish****."*

Here, Jesus is talking about people who had died unjustly, through no fault of their own, and He obviously is referring to people who literally died. Then He puts a twist on the matter, saying that His listeners will also perish if they don't repent. When will this perishing occur? One answer is that they will die soon for some unknown reason, and not from natural causes. However, the logical conclusion is that the perishing which He has in mind is in the afterlife, in which case, the parallel can only work if ultimate 'perishing' means to completely cease to exist. The people who were victims of cruelty and tragedy did not continue to live, but only in a diminished state; no, they had ceased to exist. Jesus says, "So will you, if you don't repent."

(As in other cases, some apply these verses to the destruction of Jerusalem in 70AD).

Luke 13:33-34 *"Nevertheless I must journey on today and tomorrow and the next day; for it cannot be that a prophet would* ***perish*** *outside of Jerusalem.*

Here, Jesus' meaning is clearly literal, but it applies within the history of Israel.

Luke 21:16-19 *"But you will be betrayed even by parents and brothers and relatives and friends, and they will put some of you to death, 17 and you will be hated by all because of My name. 18 "Yet not a hair of your head will* ***perish****. 19 " By your endurance you will gain your lives.*

This is a fascinating case. Notice what Jesus said: "Some of you will be put to death… but not a hair on your head will perish." The promise for protection is not within this life; Jesus just said they might die. Yet, He goes on to say they *will* be protected, so He can only mean in the afterlife, and in particular, at the judgment seat of God. The parallel is drawn between being killed in this earthly life and in the afterlife. In this life, the possible consequence of obedience is death at the hands of men; however, the reward for obedience is protection by God from destruction in judgment. In a sense, Jesus is saying we have a choice in who destroys us: men (because of obedience to God), or God (for disobedience to Him).

John 3:16 *"For God so loved the world, that He gave His only begotten Son, that whoever believes in Him shall not* ***perish****, but have eternal life.*

As we've said before, the choice presented here is

between life and death. If it was a choice between the quality of life, it could have been stated much more clearly as a choice between a life of everlasting sorrow or everlasting bliss. But this never happens. The choice is always between life and death and/or destruction.

John 10:27-29 *"My sheep hear My voice, and I know them, and they follow Me; 28 and I give eternal life to them, and they will never* ***perish****; and no one will snatch them out of My hand.*

Here is an interesting twist. Jesus says the reward for the righteous will be eternal life, and therefore they will not perish. He actually does a three-fold reinforcement: eternal life / will not perish / no one will snatch them away. He is underscoring the absolute security of this eternal life by emphasizing its permanence. This new life cannot be destroyed. Nothing can happen to it. In this case, perish can only be used literally, because a metaphoric use would not reinforce the point. If 'perish' is not literal, then Jesus' reinforcement is a moot point. What kind of promise is an unending life if life doesn't really end anyway? His whole promise is that the life He gives will not cease; if life can't cease (as with an immortal soul), what's the point of offering a non-perishable life? Should we translate this verse, "They will put you to death, but not a hair on your head will exist forever in a state of sorrow away from the glory of God"?

Acts 27:34 *"Therefore I encourage you to take some food, for this is for your preservation, for not a hair from the head of any of you will* ***perish****."*

This is Paul speaking to fellow victims of a shipwreck.

It's clearly a literal use of the word 'perish.'

> ***Romans 2:12*** *For all who have sinned without the Law will also* ***perish*** *without the Law, and all who have sinned under the Law will be judged by the Law…*

In this verse, according to traditional theology, perish is not literal, but metaphorical. This raises an important issue. Why do we automatically assume that the word 'perish' is literal when speaking about this life, but metaphorical when speaking about the afterlife? In this verse, Paul is not speaking about the here and now. He is saying that in the judgment, the law will be a moot point; whether you knew the law of Moses or not, you will be accountable for your actions. The consequence either way is that you will perish. We've been taught to assume perish in this case means to still live forever, but the case really has not been made as to why we should make this distinction.

> ***Colossians 2:20-22*** *If you have died with Christ to the elementary principles of the world, why, as if you were living in the world, do you submit yourself to decrees, such as, 21 "Do not handle, do not taste, do not touch!" 22(which all refer to things destined to* ***perish*** *with use)— in accordance with the commandments and teachings of men?*

Here again, Paul's use of the word 'perish' is literal. He is talking about food. Unless he means that food exists forever in another way. Of course, he doesn't mean this at all. He's asking why his readers are arguing about food regulations when food ceases to exist and is of no consequence.

> ***2 Peter 3:9*** *The Lord is not slow about His promise, as some count slowness, but is patient toward you, not wishing for any to* ***perish*** *but for all to come to repentance.*

Once again, the word here has to be in regards to the afterlife. When Peter says that Jesus has not returned yet because He does not want anyone to perish, he can't mean in the here and now, because we all will die, so perish has to mean at another point in time. Jesus wants people to repent so that they will not perish, and that is why He has not returned. So does 'perish' mean to cease to exist, or to exist forever in an unhappy way?

Perish (*appolluao*) is a tricky word. That it means 'to destroy' or 'to perish' is not in question. The question is how literally to take these terms. We've been taught in traditional theology to make it metaphorical, but this needs to be seriously questioned. When it speaks to the here and now, 'to perish' means to cease to exist in this life; yet when it speaks of the afterlife/judgment, it magically becomes metaphorical, with nobody explaining why there is such a critical switch in definition.

We've established that the Bible nowhere teaches the immortality of the soul; if this is the case, then how does 'perish' get interpreted to mean everlasting existence? If the soul is not immortal, then life must come from somewhere else in order for 'perish' to mean everlasting existence. When you begin with the false premise of an immortal soul, then – and only then – you have to redefine 'perish' to mean the exact opposite of what it actually means. If you begin with the Biblical view that the soul is *not* immortal, then you can let 'perish' mean what it is always supposed to mean, i.e., to be destroyed.

THE LAKE OF FIRE

This horrible place is only directly mentioned in Revelation, but it casts a shadow over the entire Bible, and indeed, fulfills all the dark warnings which are given throughout Scripture. Within the book of Revelation, it comes up twice, first as the punishment for the Devil and his knowing servants, then for the wicked who would not repent.

> ***Rev 19:20-21, 20:10*** *And the beast was seized, and with him the false prophet who performed the signs in his presence, by which he deceived those who had received the mark of the beast and those who worshiped his image; these two were thrown alive into* ***the lake of fire*** *which burns with brimstone. 21 And the rest were killed with the sword which came from the mouth of Him who sat on the horse, and all the birds were filled with their flesh.*
>
> *10 And the devil who deceived them was thrown into* ***the lake of fire and brimstone****, where the beast and the false prophet are also; and they will be tormented day and night forever and ever.*

The overall story is about a final act of rebellion. Satan is said to be bound, then released for a thousand years, which is followed by another great conflict, after which the 'ultimate rebels' are cast into the lake of fire.

While the language is mysterious and symbolic, it points one clear conclusion: that eventually God takes vengeance on those who defy Him and lead others to do the same. Their fate is said to be forever and ever. It is important to note that the word 'eternal' is not used here to describe this quality of the punishment.

Throughout Scripture, the one prevailing warning to the unrepentant is a day of fire, a destruction, a judgment. The Lake of Fire is the fulfillment of this. While it is misguided to use Revelation as the starting point for eschatology, it certainly fits in with what we've seen throughout this study. The threat of judgment, and in particular, of fire, has been prevalent for thousands of years; here, the threat is carried out.

We won't take the time to explain or interpret the rest of this passage; what we need to grasp is what is clearly stated, that the source of evil, sorrow and death is punished severely.

> ***Revelation 20:11-15*** *Then I saw a great white throne and Him who sat upon it, from whose presence earth and heaven fled away, and no place was found for them. 12 And I saw the dead, the great and the small, standing before the throne, and books were opened; and another book was opened, which is the book of life; and the dead were judged from the things which were written in the books, according to their deeds. 13 And the sea gave up the dead which were in it, and death and Hades gave up the*

> *dead which were in them; and they were judged, every one of them according to their deeds. 14 Then death and Hades were thrown into* ***the lake of fire****. This is the second death,* ***the lake of fire****. 15 And if anyone's name was not found written in the book of life, he was thrown into* ***the lake of fire****.*

This passage describes the end of history, and it occurs after the rebellion is finally and completely over. The chief rebel has been judged and punished. Within this passage, we see much that fits in with this study and completes many aspects of it. Let us make six observations.

First, notice how the defendants of the judgment are described: they are *the dead.* This is a funny way to describe humanity with its 'immortal soul.' They are not called 'the resurrected' even though they have been revived for judgment (just like Daniel 12 said). They are not called 'the languishing in a rather unpleasant mood', nor 'those living in a lesser state'. They are called "THE DEAD".

Second, notice that there are two types of books: there are several books with 'the evidence', and one book with 'the verdict'. The book of life is the determinate factor in what happens to the defendants. THE DEAD are watching someone read the Book of LIFE. It is not the 'not-so-living' reading the book of 'better-life'. It is the dead listening to the words of the Book of Life. The distinction that has dominated our study all along still holds: there is life and there is death, and nothing in between.

Third, notice where the dead come from: death and Hades, and the sea. Nobody is coming from heaven or hell. Nobody has come from a place of torment or bliss. They've come from the depository of the dead: Sheol/ Hades (and the sea). As we've said before, if people die and go to heaven or hell, this passage is a great redundancy; if we hold to the Biblical view that the deceased are still dead in the ground, then this passage fits right in. The dead are dead until they are raised for judgment.

Fourth, the Lake of Fire is the punishment for the unrepentant. All through Scripture, the chief warning has been against burning: fire & brimstone, like a blazing furnace, like chaff thrown into the flames, the fiery Gehenna, and so on. When people think of 'hell' as being a fiery, destructive place, this is not incorrect; the issue is when such a thing is manifested. The 'fires of hell' are a post-judgment phenomenon, not an experience in the 'after-life'.

This clears up a major aspect of this study: *what are we to make of the notable differences between Sheol/Hades and Gehenna?* How could Jesus speak of the fires of Gehenna, and yet it appears we lie dormant and unconscious in death? The answer is simple, if you are Biblical: we die, we lie dormant, we are raised for judgment, and the wicked are then cast into the Lake of Fire. In short, *the Lake of Fire IS Gehenna*. Sheol/Hades holds us until judgment; the wicked are then cast into Gehenna/the Lake of Fire, where the 'worm does not die, and the fire is not quenched.' Jesus said God is able to destroy both body and soul in Gehenna. He said the wicked will be like chaff in the blazing furnace.

There is no conflict between the ideas of Sheol/Hades and Gehenna. They are different places with different purposes.

Fifth, notice how the Lake of Fire is described: *the second death*. We live on this earth, and we die. After that comes judgment (Hebrews 9:27), and after that, for the unrepentant, is the Lake of Fire, the second death. We know that the first death is actual cessation of life. What is the Second Death? Is this literal, or a metaphor meaning "to exist for ever in a state of misery"? This latter view does not hold up to logic and rational thought. If the first death means to cease to exist, then in order to be 'the Second Death', it has to mean to cease to exist as well, or else it wouldn't be the 'second' one.

Those who believe in an immortal soul cannot get around this. If 'death' is only a metaphor for living forever apart from God, how does one die a second 'metaphorical' death? Keep in mind that all through Scripture, the warning has been that the wicked and unrepentant will be destroyed (or will perish); then we see the Lake of Fire being called 'the Second Death.' After all of this, how in the world can the Second Death actually mean 'to live forever in another way"? It simply doesn't work. Furthermore, the choice has always been between life and death, and here it becomes ultimately, actually true. Those who chose God receive life, those who reject Him receive death.

The original, first lie by the serpent in the Garden of Eden was "You will not die!" Here we see how untrue this deception was. The serpent's false promise was that we would possess immortality; this passage from Revelation demonstrates how utterly untrue this statement was.

Sixth, and finally, is that while Revelation says that the beast, the false prophet and the devil will be tormented forever and ever, no such thing is said here about the 'general population' who are not in the book of life. It is a mistake to assume this is the case just because such a thing was said earlier. It makes sense the 'supernatural' beings who deceived humanity and led 'the rebellion' after knowing the true God would receive a more severe judgment. This doesn't imply that the rest are innocent and undeserving of judgment, but they *are* in a lesser category of guilt.

WHAT ABOUT ETERNAL FIRE & DESTRUCTION?

One of the key words of Scripture is 'eternal' or in the Greek, *aionios*. In common usage, we often take this word to mean 'everlasting', but this is mistaken, because there is another Greek word for that *(pantote)*, and furthermore, *aionios* has a *qualitative* aspect, and not just a *quantitative*. In other words, *aionios* has to do not just with how much there is of something, but also the nature of it, as well.

As an example, somebody can say "I cleaned the entire house". They might have gone into every room and cleaned a portion of every room, but not dusted or vacuumed. Another person might say, "I scrubbed the whole house from top to bottom" and you know that they cleaned not only the entire house, but cleaned it thoroughly. This gives you an idea about *aionios.* When something is said of *aionios* fire, it is not necessarily saying "a fire that lasts forever". It is saying that the fire is *utterly thorough.* In other words, it's going to really get the job done.

But there is more. In the Greek, *aionios* literally means 'of the age.' This is fascinating, because it fits in very well with our framework. We started this study by establishing the ideas of This Age and The Age to Come. It is interesting that the "fire of the age" takes place in the Age to Come. Furthermore, realize that the word 'aionios' is also used of life, and gets translated as "eternal life". People usually take this to mean that this new life is everlasting; but it can also mean "life of the Age". It can also mean 'a very deep and rich life' as well.

The following are the best known examples of 'eternal fire':

> ***Matthew 18:8*** *" If your hand or your foot causes you to stumble, cut it off and throw it from you; it is better for you to enter life crippled or lame, than to have two hands or two feet and be cast into the* ***eternal fire****.*
>
> ***Matthew 25:41-42*** *"Then He will also say to those on His left, 'Depart from Me, accursed ones, into the* ***eternal fire*** *which has been prepared for the devil and his angels;*

Notice in the above cases, that the fire is said to have been prepared for the devil and his angels, but those who have rejected the offer of life from God are cast into it as penalty for their rebellion.

> ***Matthew 25:45-46*** *"Then He will answer them, 'Truly I say to you, to the extent that you did not do it to one of the least of these, you did not do it to Me.' 46 "These will go away into* ***eternal punishment****, but the righteous into* ***eternal life****."*

Notice the contrast is between punishment and life, and both are said to be 'of the age' or utterly thorough.

> ***2 Thessalonians 1:9-10*** *These will pay the penalty of* ***eternal destruction****, away from the presence of the Lord and from the glory of His power, 10 when He comes to be glorified in His saints on that day,*

> ***Jude 6-7*** *And angels who did not keep their own domain, but abandoned their proper abode, He has kept in eternal bonds under darkness for the judgment of the great day, 7 just as Sodom and Gomorrah and the cities around them, since they in the same way as these indulged in gross immorality and went after strange flesh, are exhibited as an example in undergoing the punishment of* ***eternal fire****.*

Two different authors use *aionios* in reference to punishment, and both in light of the Day of Yahweh. Notice that Sodom and Gomorrah's punishment is said to be 'eternal' as an example for us.

Having said that, the following cases are also very interesting:

> ***Mark 3:28-30*** *"Truly I say to you, all sins shall be forgiven the sons of men, and whatever blasphemies they utter; 29 but whoever blasphemes against the Holy Spirit never has forgiveness, but is guilty of an* ***eternal sin****" —*

Hebrews 5:9-10 *And having been made perfect, He became to all those who obey Him the source of* ***eternal salvation****, 10 being designated by God as a high priest according to the order of Melchizedek.*

Hebrews 6:1-2 *Therefore leaving the elementary teaching about the Christ, let us press on to maturity, not laying again a foundation of repentance from dead works and of faith toward God, 2 of instruction about washings and laying on of hands, and the resurrection of the dead and* ***eternal judgment****.*

Hebrews 9:11-12 *But when Christ appeared as a high priest of the good things to come, He entered through the greater and more perfect tabernacle, not made with hands, that is to say, not of this creation; 12 and not through the blood of goats and calves, but through His own blood, He entered the holy place once for all, having obtained* ***eternal redemption****.*

All of the examples above have one thing in common: *aionios* is used to describe something that happened just once, but the effect of which is permanently enduring. Jesus says blaspheming the Holy Spirit is an *aionios* sin; Hebrews says that salvation, redemption and judgment are all *aionios*. Each of these happened (or happens) just once, but each are permanent in their results. This lends one more shade to the deeper meaning of 'Eternal.'

"Eternal", or *aionios*, then has all these connotations: of the age; deeply effective; permanent, and not just 'everlasting', which again, is another word in the Greek (*pantote*). This word is found in 1 Thess. 4:17 and Hebrews 7:25.

CONCLUSIONS

We've covered a lot of territory, but what we saw all pointed to the same thing: that just as the Old Testament repeatedly warned that the wicked and unrepentant would be destroyed, the New Testament also pointed to this harsh reality. In the Old Testament, the meaning clearly could not be referring to This Age, because as the Hebrew Scriptures repeatedly lament, the wicked actually succeed and prosper quite a bit. The destruction of the wicked was clearly in reference to The Age to Come. Likewise, the New Testament clearly points to a destructive judgment in another age, and not in this age, and not upon death.

First, Gehenna is a different place than Hades. Where Hades is a place of unconscious non-existence, Gehenna is a place of fire and torment. Both fire and undying worms are associated with this place.

Second, Whereas Sheol/Hades is a place of natural, earthly decay, Gehenna is a place of being consumed and destroyed as a result of judgment in the afterlife. Using hyperbole, Jesus warned that it is better to dismember yourself rather than have your entire being destroyed in Gehenna. Furthermore, Jesus said that God is able to destroy both body and soul there.

Third, Jesus repeatedly warned that in the judgment, there would be weeping and gnashing of teeth. This points to a conscious suffering in judgment, but says nothing about it being everlasting. Furthermore, weeping and gnashing are associated both with fire and outer darkness, and judgment. The purpose of these warnings is to prevent ghastly regret and cause a person to repent and submit to God.

Fourth, the word 'perishing' (or 'perish') is best understood literally. In This Age, 'perish' most often clearly means to die, to cease existing; and yet when used in regards to judgment in the after-life, traditional theology makes a unwarranted switch and makes 'perish' a metaphor. The result of this is to cause 'perish' to mean the exact opposite of what it normally means. People are forced to do this because they begin with the false premise of the immortality of the soul. If one retains the Biblical teaching that the soul is *not* immortal, then no radical change of definition is necessary.

Fifth, Gehenna is the result of judgment and the consequence is fire. It is called the second death, which is impossible to render as a metaphor. The people who await judgment are called 'the dead' and are brought up from death and Hades for judgment, just as we've established earlier. In light of all this, the logical conclusion is to consider the Lake of Fire to be the same thing as Gehenna, which Jesus portrayed as a place of judgment and torment.

Sixth, we have seen that the word 'eternal' is misunderstood and perhaps mis-translated. It is literally Greek for "of the age" which fits the motifs of This Age and The Age to Come perfectly. It also has a connotation of utter thoroughness, and permanence. To render the word 'eternal' as meaning 'everlasting' is hasty and misguided. It is a far richer word, and a far more significant word than one that speaks only of how long something lasts.

11

The New Jerusalem

One of my favorite hymns growing up was "This World Is Not My Home." The message was pretty clear, that someday in God's time, I would go away to "somewhere beyond the blue." The earth was just a temporary inconvenience. Ironically, I never noticed the clash between that hymn and another favorite, "This Is My Father's World." The end of that hymn says that eventually Jesus will be satisfied and that "earth and heav'n [will] be one." These are two very different sets of expectations.

This chapter deals with the central question: "Where will we spend eternity?" If you grew up the USA attending an Evangelical church, most likely your response will be, "Why in heaven, of course!". Like much else in traditional theology, I held this view at one time, but no longer. Instead, I've come to see that despite much pop theology, the Bible does not point us in the direction of a heavenly home "out there somewhere", but towards an eternity lived in a redeemed, renewed earth. For many, this idea will seem like a stunning leap out of nowhere, but as we will see in the course of this chapter, life forever on earth is very much the Biblical expectation.

A GLARING OMISSION

I'd like you to consider something: if indeed the chief objective of Christian faith is to die and go to heaven, doesn't it follow that this idea would be prominent in the teachings of Scripture? Think of all the hymns, songs, sermons and expressions you've heard about eternity. If your upbringing was like mine, dying and going to heaven was the main point of it all.

Is it not odd, then, that with this being the most important idea of Christian faith that *the Bible nowhere says that Christians die and go to heaven?* This idea seems to be implied by some verses (see chapter 4), but there is *no* verse that actually says this.

Jesus and Paul both repeatedly mention the resurrection, judgment, the wrath of God, immortality, eternal life; but *not once* do they say that we die and go to heaven. As Christians, we have gotten used to seeing it this way, but honest and thorough reflection will bear this point out: we've been taught to see something that isn't there.

Out of the different facets in this study, this is for me the least obvious one. There are some verses (which we will immediately look at) that seem to hold up the popular view that all creation is destroyed, but eventually we will find that weight of Scripture points to earth being our eternal home.

THE CONTRARIAN PASSAGES

In previous sections, I've admitted when there is a difficulty in my argument; I will do so again here with the three passages which do seem to point in the opposite direction of my findings. We will see that one of these passages apparently seems to point in two directions at once.

Isaiah 65:17-18 *"For behold, I create a new heavens and a new earth;*

And the former things will not be remembered or come to mind.

18 "But be glad and rejoice forever in what I create;

For behold, I create Jerusalem for rejoicing and her people for gladness.

Isa 66:22-24 *"For just as the new heavens and the new earth*

Which I make will endure before Me," declares the LORD,

"So your offspring and your name will endure.

23 "And it shall be from new moon to new moon and from sabbath to sabbath,

All mankind will come to bow down before Me," says the LORD.

24 "Then they will go forth and look on the corpses of the men

Who have transgressed against Me.

For their worm will not die and their fire will not be quenched;

And they will be an abhorrence to all mankind."

2 Peter 3:10-13 *But the day of the Lord will come like a thief, in which the heavens will pass away with a roar and the elements will be destroyed with intense heat, and the earth and its works will be burned up.*

11 Since all these things are to be destroyed in this way, what sort of people ought you to be in holy conduct and godliness, 12 looking for and hastening the coming of the day of God, because of which the heavens will be destroyed by burning, and the elements will melt with intense heat! 13 But according to His promise we are looking for new heavens and a new earth, in which righteousness dwells.

As we've said, the first and most logical interpretation of all these verses would be to take them at face value and say that creation as we know it will pass, to be replaced with an undefiled new creation. Another interpretation one could hold is that these verses are metaphors and hyperbole, as when a prophet says that the whole earth will be shaken, etc.

Having said that, let's return and notice something about Isaiah 65:17ff. Look what is said after the statement of vs. 17:

Isaiah 65:20-23 *"No longer will there be in it an infant who lives but a few days,*

Or an old man who does not live out his days;

For the youth will die at the age of one hundred

And the one who does not reach the age of one hundred will be thought accursed.

21 "They will build houses and inhabit them;

They will also plant vineyards and eat their fruit.

22 "They will not build and another inhabit, they will not plant and another eat;

For as the lifetime of a tree, so will be the days of My people,

And My chosen ones will wear out the work of their hands.

23 "They will not labor in vain, Or bear children for calamity;

For they are the offspring of those blessed by the LORD,

and their descendants with them.

What is being conveyed by these subsequent verses is about life on earth, *only with much longer life spans.* When and how will these be fulfilled? The description points to something greater than has been experienced yet in history. Sometimes the prophets speak very glowingly about life after the Babylonian exile with such hyperbole, but that doesn't fit here. This passage makes two things very clear. First, that this life is *earthly*, and second, that it is life at a level which is not currently enjoyed. (But note that death still seems to be on the scene, though!).

So there we have a confusing set of ideas. I think the safest and best explanation is that verses such as these are pointing to a renewed earth, in reference to having been cleansed of corruption and evil. We will see in the next section that there is good reason for this interpretation.

In California, you can go up and down the state and visit 21 Spanish missions, built in the 18th century by Franciscan padres. In some cases, you find that what they call 'restored' is practically rebuilt from scratch. Pictures show desolate ruins before efforts began to reclaim this part of the state's heritage. Likewise, I believe that the verses referring to a new heavens and a new earth could be interpreted in the same way. Things will be so restored and so renewed that it could seem like they were made from scratch. With that in mind, let us look at the relevant passages.

THE LIBERATION OF CREATION

Some passages talk of creation being restored, such as the following.

> ***Psalm 102:25-28*** *"Of old You founded the earth,*
> *And the heavens are the work of Your hands.*
> *26 "Even they will perish, but You endure; and all of them will wear out like a garment;*
> *Like clothing You will change them and they will be changed.*
> *27 "But You are the same, and Your years will not come to an end.*
> *28 "The children of Your servants will continue,*
> *And their descendants will be established before You."*

Notice the mixed message in Psalm 102. On the one hand, it says that heavens and earth will perish; on the other hand, it says they will be changed like a person changes clothes. This reinforces the point made above that "New

Heavens" language can mean rejuvenation. Also, immortality is pointed at; God is immortal, and *as a result* of His immortality, so shall His children be.

> ***Acts 3:19-22*** *"Therefore repent and return, so that your sins may be wiped away, in order that times of refreshing may come from the presence of the Lord; 20 and that He may send Jesus, the Christ appointed for you, 21 whom heaven must receive until the period of restoration of all things about which God spoke by the mouth of His holy prophets from ancient time.*

"Period of restoration" is not mentioned anywhere else in Scripture, yet according to Peter, it is an idea that the prophets had been saying since the beginning. What is this restoration? We are not told, but the fact that "all things" is the object of restoration, it makes sense that complete renewal of creation is in view.

> ***Romans 8:18-23*** *For I consider that the sufferings of this present time are not worthy to be compared with the glory that is to be revealed to us. 19 For the anxious longing of the creation waits eagerly for the revealing of the sons of God. 20 For the creation was subjected to futility, not willingly, but because of Him who subjected it, in hope 21 that the creation itself also will be set free from its slavery to corruption into the freedom of the glory of the children of God. 22 For we know that the whole creation groans and suffers the pains of childbirth together until now. 23 And not only this, but also we ourselves, having the first fruits of the Spirit, even we ourselves groan within ourselves, waiting eagerly for our adoption as sons, the redemption of our body.*

Paul's theology here is sweeping, and is the clearest

declaration of God restoring creation. Notice four things: First, creation is waiting for the sons of God to be revealed. When will that happen? The obvious and logical answer is on the Day of Yahweh, or Judgment Day. What Paul meant by creation being subjected to futility could be debated, but its totality is clearly in mind. Second, the result of the revealing of the sons of God is the *liberation* of creation. Consider this: if all the cosmos and creation are supposed to be destroyed and replaced, what would be the point of liberating it first? It would be like releasing prisoners from a concentration camp and then gunning them down as they left the gates. No, creation is waiting to be set free from the brokenness of sinful rebellion.

Third, what analogy does Paul use of this liberation? *Childbirth.* Creation is groaning and suffering awaiting the issue of something new from itself. This analogy points again to a *renewed* earth. If Paul was thinking of heaven and earth being destroyed, the logical metaphor would be to say "creation is groaning on its deathbed." Fourth, and finally, notice how Paul ties in the redemption of our body with the liberation of creation. This is prime resurrection talk. Just as he anticipated the renewal of our physical bodies, so too, it would seem, Paul anticipates a 'resurrection body' for earth and creation. We are subject to decay; earth is subject to decay. We are waiting for renewal in the Day of Yahweh; earth is waiting for renewal.

The idea that creation is to be redeemed and restored

into a new glory is not a leap away from Biblical teaching but is contained within Scripture. In the beginning, God said "It is good" and when He did, He meant it far more than we realize. *God truly loves His creation, and wants it redeemed.*

Special Case: Matt 19:28

> *And Jesus said to them, "Truly I say to you, that you who have followed Me,* ***in the regeneration*** *when the Son of Man will sit on His glorious throne, you also shall sit upon twelve thrones, judging the twelve tribes of Israel.*

In only this one place in the New Testament, Jesus seems to point to something along this line. With no further explanation, He speaks of a 'regeneration'. He does not elaborate what He means or what it is that is being regenerated. It is entirely reasonable that He is referring to a renewal of all creation itself.

INHERIT THE LAND

One of the primary concerns of Old Testament Jews was their tie to the land which God promised them. The relationship of God to Israel was always seen via the situation of the land. God's promises to Abraham included the land of the Canaanites. When Israel went to Egypt, the promise was a return to the land. After they returned to the land, their faithlessness was punished by invasions by surrounding countries into the land. When Israel would not repent, they were thrown into exile away from the land. When this happened, God said that they would be gathered from the globe and returned to the land. 2,000 years after Rome destroyed Jerusalem, the Jews received the land *again* in 1948.

Furthermore, the land was carefully divided up among the tribes of Israel, and the family genealogies were important because they assured that people could retain the land in the Jubilee years, when property was returned to the original families.

So, the land was important to the Jews.

Within that historical reality, there is also the spiritual aspect: the Jews believed that the righteous would remain on the land and the wicked would perish. So there is a specific and general principle at work here. On the one level, there was the matter of the individual retaining legal rights to the land which was in his family. On another level, there was the idea that the wicked would be taken away from the land so as to end its defilement by their sin. With that in mind, let us look at the following passages.

> **Psalm 37:8-11** *Cease from anger and forsake wrath;*
> *Do not fret; it leads only to evildoing.*
> *9 For evildoers will be cut off, but those who wait for the LORD, they will inherit the land.*
> *10 Yet a little while and the wicked man will be no more;*
> *And you will look carefully for his place and he will not be there.*
> *11 But the humble will inherit the land and will delight themselves in abundant prosperity.*

If you read through this entire Psalm you will see the phrase, "inherit the land" several more times in verses 22, 29 and 34. It is the refrain of the Psalm, giving a promise that God will not overlook their faithfulness. The question arises: when is this fulfilled? Yes, it should have been fulfilled by observing the law of Jubilee in the Old Testament, but we don't know that Israel ever carried it out. God has made a promise that the righteous will inherit the land.

So, a key question: is this fulfilled in This Age, or in The Age to Come? Life in this age is replete with examples of people who have been cheated of what is rightfully theirs (1 Kings 21). In reality, *the righteous are ripped off all the time!* So the righteous and innocent are *supposed* to be rewarded by prosperity, but we know this doesn't always hold true. This promise is to be fulfilled in the Age to Come.

> ***Psalm 115:16-18*** *The heavens are the heavens of the LORD,*
>
> *But* ***the earth He has given to the sons of men.***
>
> *17 The dead do not praise the LORD, nor do any who go down into silence;*
>
> *18 But as for us, we will bless the LORD from this time forth and forever.*
>
> *Praise the LORD!*

This Psalm states the obvious, that the heavens are the Lord's and the earth is the domain of humanity. But notice something peculiar: the dead do not praise God, but the righteous will praise God forever, and *by implication*, they will do so on the earth. Several of the main points of this study are contained right here: The dead are unconscious but there is a resurrection of the righteous.

> ***Proverbs 10:3*** *The righteous will never be shaken,* ***but the wicked will not dwell in the land.***

Again, this promise is one that we cannot take to be fulfilled in This Age. The righteous are run over, tossed and shaken all the time, and the wicked get away with murder and often prosper (Psalm 73). Again, that the wicked will not dwell in the land points to a fulfillment not in the here and now but someday. And, if this is true, then the fulfillment is that the righteous live *on earth, in the land.*

> ***Matthew 5:5*** *"Blessed are the gentle, for they shall inherit the earth.*

When Jesus began the Beatitudes with this promise, He was on familiar territory, as we saw from the above passages. Jesus spoke to people whose land was overrun by a pagan army from Rome, and apparently had their homes stolen by Pharisees (Mark 12:40). His audience was used to oppression, high taxes, and so on. Once again, the promise is for another age, for in This Age, it all too often does not hold true.

Some have taken the above passages (and many similar in sentiment) and said that these kinds of promises will be fulfilled in the Millennium. This conclusion is somewhat logical. It comes in part from the realization that life is very often unjust and unfair; therefore the promise has to be fulfilled at some other time. That conclusion, I agree with; however, I think the idea of the Millennium is misguided.

Consider this: how much is actually said about the Millennium? The truth is, *very little.* More than this, *the word is not in the Bible,* yet we have built a lot of theology upon it. There are eight times when 'a thousand years' is mentioned, and they are all in 2 Peter and Revelation. In the case of 2 Peter, he is commenting that a "thousand years is like a day" to God, which has nothing to do with the popular concept of the Millennium. That leaves six mentions, all in Revelation 20. With no other foundation than this highly symbolic and mysterious passage, contemporary Christians have built a flimsy house of cards which we call "The Millennium." This is poor and sloppy theology making. Seminars, books and sermons have all focused upon something which is almost a cipher in Scripture.

Consider this: if the Millennium was such a focal point of God's plan, wouldn't have Jesus and Paul mentioned it *at least once?* Again, they both talk of resurrection, judgment, eternal life, and destruction, but not once do either of them say a thing about any so-called 'Millennium.' Whatever the thousand years of Revelation 20 is, it is *not* something to put at the center of eschatology.

Having said that, then the great descriptive passages of mountains dripping with wine and every person sitting under their fig tree, and the lion lying down with the lamb can be taken in two ways. Either they are hyperbole speaking of events in This Age, or they are in reference to a glorious life in The Age to Come. They need not be exclusively one or the other. But it is a big mistake to assign them to something which is mentioned only six times in one chapter out of the whole Bible.

ONE WILL BE LEFT…

In Matthew 24, there is a passage that those who hold to rapture theology use to bolster their belief:

> ***Matthew 24:38-41*** *"For as in those days before the flood they were eating and drinking, marrying and giving in marriage, until the day that Noah entered the ark, 39 and they did not understand until the flood came and took them all away; so will the coming of the Son of Man be. 40 "Then there will be two men in the field;* ***one will be taken*** *and one will be left. 41 " Two women will be grinding at the mill;* ***one will be taken*** *and one will be left.*

In reading this passage, many have been taught that this is about the 'Rapture' and how the righteous will be snatched away to heaven, leaving the wicked on earth for judgment. However, this is the complete opposite of the Jewish expectation for Divine justice. From their point of view, the ones left behind would be the righteous, and the wicked would be removed from God's creation.

This might seem like a radical re-interpretation, but the passage itself does not say who is taken and who is left, so rapture theologians cannot claim this as solid support in light of the rest of the Biblical witness.

KINGDOMS OF THE WORLD AND OF GOD

When Jesus prayed "Your will be done on earth as it is in heaven…", He was not introducing a new idea to His listeners. The Kingdom of God concept had ancient roots in Hebrew culture. This topic is much too large to delve into here, and merits a volume all its own; having said that, it is still an important part of this study, so we must touch on it.

The key point we want to address is this: when the prophets, Jesus and the Jews referred to the Kingdom of God, where was it that they expected it to be? Because of pop theology and hasty conclusions, we often conclude that the Kingdom of God is an other-worldly experience, and it is understandable as to why this is so. When Pilate was interrogating Jesus, the Savior stated that His kingdom was "not of this world." The immediate and apparent meaning is that it is located in another realm or world.

But was this what Jesus was saying at that point? I think not. His point in that context was that His power base and support was not going to be through armies or popular uprisings, but through divine power. The Jews, too, believed that there would be a day when God intervened for good and secured the land for the righteous and removed the wicked from it. These thoughts are in parallel. The Jews waited for the day of God's kingdom to burst forth from heaven, and Jesus essentially said the same thing to Pilate. With this in mind, let's look at the relevant passages.

> ***Daniel 2:44-45*** *"In the days of those kings the God of heaven will set up a* ***kingdom which will never be destroyed****, and that kingdom will not be left for another people; it will crush and put an end to all these kingdoms,* ***but it will itself endure forever****. 45 "Inasmuch as you saw that a stone was cut out of the mountain without hands and that it crushed the iron, the bronze, the clay, the silver and the gold, the great God has made known to the king what will take place in the future; so the dream is true and its interpretation is trustworthy."*

Having interpreted king Nebuchadnezzar's dream, Daniel tells him that there will be earthly kingdoms established: Babylon, Persia/Greece, and then Rome. After these earthly kingdoms, God's kingdom will come and supplant all the earthly reigns which have been established. For good reason, the Jews expected God's kingdom to wipe out the Romans when Jesus appeared to be the Messiah. Thus Jesus had the job of explaining that the kingdom of God *had* arrived, but would co-exist with the pagan powers for a while. This was the purpose of his kingdom parables of Matthew 13, to show that this heavenly kingdom would be quiet and subtle in its arrival, not overwhelming and obvious.

> ***Daniel 7:13-14*** *"I kept looking in the night visions, and behold, with the clouds of heaven One like a Son of Man was coming, And He came up to the Ancient of Days and was presented before Him. 14 "And to Him was given dominion, glory and a kingdom, that all the peoples, nations and men of every language might serve Him. His dominion is an everlasting dominion which will not pass away; and His kingdom is one which will not be destroyed.*

> ***Daniel 7:27*** *'Then the sovereignty, the dominion and the greatness of all the kingdoms under the whole heaven will be given to the people of the saints of the Highest One; His kingdom will be an everlasting kingdom, and all the dominions will serve and obey Him.'*

In both of these passages, Daniel is making note of the earthly kingdoms which are to come in the future, and then concludes with celebrating the arrival of God's kingdom. This much is obvious. The part which seems to go neglected is that the expectation is that this great coming kingdom *is on earth.* One reasonable conclusion is that Jesus fulfilled this in His coming, and indeed He did; however, it does not follow automatically that this kingdom is subsequently transferred to heaven in place of earth. To state it another way: when Jesus appeared on the scene it was indeed the arrival of the kingdom of God, *but it was not the complete realization of it.* The expectation rendered by Daniel is that the earthly kingdoms of the world will be swallowed up by the kingdom of God *upon earth.* This was not fulfilled completely by Jesus. His kingdom arrived, but it did not and has not yet reached its full force.

The main point of all this is that the Jewish expectation was that a Messiah would usher in the kingdom of God above and against the corrupt pagan kingdoms. The reason that Jesus kept His identity as Messiah secret was that there would be a rush by His followers to inaugurate the kingdom right here and now, and that was not His intent. People usually get this point correct but then go on to a false conclusion, that the kingdom would be located in heaven. The Jewish expectation for an earth bound kingdom of God was correct; it was *the timing* which was off. Jesus *did* come to establish the kingdom of God on earth; *just not at that time.*

Consider the following passage:

> ***1 Corinthians 15:27-28*** *For HE HAS PUT ALL THINGS IN SUBJECTION UNDER HIS FEET. But when He says, "All things are put in subjection," it is evident that He is excepted who put all things in subjection to Him. 28 When all things are subjected to Him, then the Son Himself also will be subjected to the One who subjected all things to Him, so that God may be all in all.*

Notice how this directly parallels Daniel 7:13 & 14: a supernatural figure given the reign over all kingdoms. The Son of Man is then presented to the Ancient of Days. It is no coincidence that this passage comes from the fullest treatment concerning the resurrection. The kingdom of God coming to earth in the book of Daniel is fulfilled by the Day of Yahweh, which includes the resurrection. Notice in Daniel how it says the kingdoms of earth will be given over to the saints. And these saints *are upon the earth.*

We can see this train of thought elsewhere:

> ***Revelation 5:9-10*** *And they sang a new song, saying, "Worthy are You to take the book and to break its seals; for You were slain, and purchased for God with Your blood men from every tribe and tongue and people and nation. 10 "You have made*

them to be a kingdom and priests to our God; and they will reign upon the earth."

Revelation 11:15-17 *Then the seventh angel sounded; and there were loud voices in heaven, saying, "The kingdom of the world has become the kingdom of our Lord and of His Christ; and He will reign forever and ever." 16 And the twenty-four elders, who sit on their thrones before God, fell on their faces and worshiped God…*

In both of these cases, these verses parallel the passages from Daniel, saying that the earthly kingdoms will be overcome and absorbed by the kingdom of God, and the location of this event is clearly earth. It is obvious that this has not yet been fulfilled, so it is a question of when it is supposed to be fulfilled. We could take several approaches to this.

We could say it is hyperbolic and/or metaphoric language, and the Christian church has actually fulfilled this prophecy. I find this hard to believe that the ongoing chaos and tragedy of life is supposed to continue on side by side with the ultimate and total victory of God. Therefore, it is a mistake to conclude that it has been completely fulfilled already.

Some say that this is fulfilled by the Millennium, when the saints rule over earth but only temporarily. We have eliminated this concept as a legitimate theological factor. Whatever is meant by Revelation's idea of the thousand years, we can't build too much upon it.

Another point of view is that the coming kingdom of God is a mandate to Christians to overtake and subdue the current political structures and act as God's stewards in the here and now. This notion has frightened many people and rightly so. Having pastored several churches now, I wouldn't trust us to run a pet shop.

The best and safest conclusion is that the promises of God's earthly reign over all kingdoms is in the future at a time of His choosing, not ours. The resurrected Messiah will be King of Kings in deed as well as in title in the Age to Come.

THE NEW JERUSALEM

Long before John wrote Revelation 21, the idea of a New Jerusalem had already been established:

> ***Zechariah 14:6-11*** *In that day there will be no light; the luminaries will dwindle. 7 For it will be a unique day which is known to the LORD, neither day nor night, but it will come about that at evening time there will be light. 8 <u>And in that day living waters will flow out of Jerusalem</u>, half of them toward the eastern sea and the other half toward the western sea; it will be in summer as well as in winter. 9 <u>And the LORD will be king over all the earth</u>; in that day the LORD will be the only one, and His name the only one.*
>
> *10 All the land will be changed into a plain from Geba to Rimmon south of* ***Jerusalem****; but* ***Jerusalem*** *will rise and remain on its site from Benjamin's Gate as far as the place of the First Gate to the Corner Gate, and from the Tower of Hananel to the king's wine presses. 11 People will live in it, and <u>there will no longer be a curse</u>, for* ***Jerusalem*** *will dwell in security.*

This passage comes from the middle of a description where a cataclysmic battle is being fought over Jerusalem, something which is echoed in Daniel and Revelation. All of these passages merit further in-depth exploration and discussion, but I wish to make just one point: the prophecy of Jerusalem is clearly located on earth, and it says that God *will* be king over all the earth. As Christians, we believe that God is now currently King of all creation but the point underscored here is that His reign is mitigated by His own choosing until the day when the kingdom of God reaches its full extent in the Age to Come.

With this in mind, we come to our final passage:

> ***Revelation 21:1-6*** *Then I saw a new heaven and a new*
> *earth; for the first heaven and the first earth passed away, and there*
> *is no longer any sea. 2 And I saw the holy city, new Jerusalem,*
> *coming down out of heaven from God, made ready as a bride*
> *adorned for her husband. 3 And I heard a loud voice from the*
> *throne, saying, "Behold, the tabernacle of God is among men, and*
> *He will dwell among them, and they shall be His people, and God*
> *Himself will be among them, 4 and He will wipe away every tear*
> *from their eyes; and there will no longer be any death; there will no*
> *longer be any mourning, or crying, or pain; the first things have*
> *passed away." 5 And He who sits on the throne said, "Behold,*
> *I am making all things new." And He said, "Write, for these*
> *words are faithful and true."*

We wrap up this section with a statement that seems to contradict the main point I've been trying to make. Verse 1 says there will be a new heaven and new earth, for the first ones have passed away. But notice that verse 5 shows God saying that He makes all things new. This points to the idea that we are talking about: a *renewed earth and heaven.* It is renewed because God will finally be in complete unchallenged sovereignty over creation. Notice when this takes place: after creation has been purged of evil (Revelation 19).

Also notice that this New Jerusalem comes down from heaven, obviously implying that it is coming down *to earth.* This would be exactly what Daniel depicted, and what Jesus prayed for in the Lord's prayer: *"Your kingdom come, Your will be done, <u>on earth</u>, as it is in heaven."* This was not a random, casual phrase in Jesus' prayer; it was the re-affirmation of what He and His fellow Jews were anticipating throughout their history.

CONCLUSIONS

<u>First</u>**,** the Bible actually does not say anything about dying and going to heaven. If this really is the main point of the Christian faith, it certainly is strange that nothing is directly said on the subject. It is never said in the Old Testament, and Jesus and Paul never utter the phrase "die and go to heaven." It simply isn't there.

<u>Second</u>**,** we have noted several passages which clearly expect a glorious future here upon the earth. How to interpret these passages can be varied, but the best solution is to take them at face value that there will indeed be a actual, physical and glorious existence upon earth free from

sorrow, death and injustice. We have shown that using the so-called Millennium is an insufficient answer to this. If the Millennium was a vital aspect of God's plan, it's strange that is only mentioned in one chapter out of the whole Bible. In light of the rest of Scripture, it seems ill-advised to build much upon the idea of the Millennium.

Third, we established that the Jews fully expected God to come and redeem His people *on earth* and that there is nothing in subsequent revelation to reject this view. They expected God's kingdom to overpower and absorbed the earthly kingdoms. When Jesus spoke of His kingdom, He never said that it is *in heaven*; nor did He say that this is the final destination of His people. Indeed, the Lord's Prayer clearly asks for the kingdom of Heaven to come *to earth,* just as Daniel predicted and as His fellow Jews hoped for.

Fourth, we have seen that there is good reason to believe that creation will not be destroyed and discarded, but rather liberated and renewed by God's power in His time. While there are some passages that seem to indicate the destruction of all creation, there are clearer statements pointing to renewal. At the end of the Biblical story, we see God saying "Behold, I make all things new", and not "all new things".

Fifth, there are repeated promises that the righteous will inherit the land throughout the Old Testament, and Jesus Himself said the meek shall inherit the earth. These have not and cannot be fulfilled while evil and sin have power in creation. If creation is destroyed and we all go to heaven, as pop theology dictates, *then these are false promises.* The meek and lowly get run over all the time in this world; to say that they shall inherit the land and/or earth and then destroy it would be a glaring inconsistency.

This IS our Father's world, and IT IS our home. Forever.

12

The Tree of Life Returns

The story has now come full circle. The Biblical history of humanity began in the Garden of Eden, with the Tree of Life being the centerpiece. This tree was the great hope for immortality but it was lost; still, the story went on to include promises of immortality, first in little hints, then in direct and specific language.

The story was always about life. God looked over His creation and it was good. He loved what He made, and He wanted it to live forever, but rebellion cut the cord. God wanted us to live forever, and we want to live forever. The great heresy of all existence is the idea that we can live forever without God sustaining us. An even greater travesty is that well meaning Christians adopt the hubristic belief in an immortal soul, not realizing that this is the ultimate self flattery that defies God.

With that in mind, let's turn to our final passage for consideration.

> ***Revelation 22:1-5*** *Then he showed me a river of the* *__water of life__*, *clear as crystal, coming from the throne of God and of the Lamb, 2 in the middle of its street. On either side of the river was* ***the tree of life***, *bearing twelve kinds of fruit, yielding its fruit every month;* *__and the leaves of the tree were for the healing of the nations__*. *3 There will no longer be any curse; and the throne of God and of the Lamb will be in it, and His bond-servants will serve Him; 4 they will see His face, and His name will be on their foreheads. 5 And there will no longer be any night; and they will not have need of the light of a lamp nor the light of the sun, because the Lord God will illumine them;* *__and they will reign forever and ever.__*

To start with, we need to acknowledge that all of this is being portrayed with the symbolic language that is used throughout Revelation. The New Jerusalem is a symbol of the new, sinless society which God will create in the Age to Come.

Having said that, we will focus on just one point in this passage: this is the first time since Genesis 3 that the Tree of Life is mentioned (apart from Proverbs 3:18, 11:30, 13:12 and 15:4, which are speaking of something else entirely).

It is entirely fitting that this should be the case. Remember the story in Genesis. Adam and Eve sinned; God's intervention after that was to drive them away from the Garden, thus cutting off access to the Tree of Life.

The purpose for this is made very clear: to prevent Adam & Eve *from* living forever. As we said in chapter one, the implication is very clear: without the Tree of Life, *there is no living forever.* It would be strange for God to say that their immortality must be prevented if in fact we had immortal souls and could live forever.

Most Christians get the theology half right: they say God had to cut off the Tree of Life because now that the human race was corrupted by sin and God did not want us to live forever in the defiled condition. Then they go on to say we have immortal souls. *This makes no sense!* It is far more logical and consistent to say that in 'losing' the Tree of Life, we lost the chance for immortality.

This being the case, then the timing of the return of the Tree of Life is most significant: the Tree of Life returns *after* the devil, sin and evil are purged from creation in the Lake of Fire (the second death). We can not receive immortality until the rebellion that lost it is ended. In the Lake of Fire, God removes the contaminants and contagion that corrupted creation; once that is done, *then* immortality can be allowed; otherwise, the same conditions of Genesis 3 would still be in effect.

The Biblical story is about how God created us for life and immortality and how it was lost. Then a gracious God provided a second chance through the Resurrection of Jesus of Nazareth, the Messiah of Israel. The verses about the Tree of Life are the 'bookends' of that story. Really, I think it can be said that the Tree of Life *IS* the story.

Part Three Summary

In Part Three, we saw many false ideas of pop theology overturned by Biblical teachings. While this may be confusing for some, the reality is that many people are victims of slipshod study and simplistic interpretations of Scripture. Furthermore, because of this hasty 'theologizing', we lose the unity of the Bible in its overall message. There are 13 important points to Part Three of this study:

1. Repeatedly, the Old Testament says that the wicked will be destroyed. Sometimes this is in direct connection to the judgment, oftentimes it is just a statement without explanation.
2. Oftentimes, when we are told of the fate of the wicked, it is paired with a promise of life or prosperity for the righteous. Many people take these warnings (or promises) for life in the here and now, but life shows us over and over again that it rarely works this way. The wicked often triumph, the poor consistently are oppressed and left in poverty, and good righteous people are frequently persecuted.
3. Since the destruction of the wicked is repeatedly and consistently given throughout the Old Testament, the best interpretation of these warnings is that this punishment is carried out at a future time, and not in This Age.
4. Nothing in the Old Testament points to an everlast-

ing punishment at another locale in the after-life. The verdict is always described in final and permanent terms ("The wicked will be no more").

5. In chapter 2, we saw that the Old Testament points to death as being final, with no continuing existence of any kind. The destruction of the wicked in chapter 9 is entirely in keeping with this.
6. Ezekiel 18 repeatedly states that the wicked soul who will not repent will die, while the righteous person shall live. Being that both the wicked and the righteous do their deeds in this life and continue to live, it follows that the phrases "that soul shall die" and "that soul shall live" apply to the Age to Come, and not in This Age.
7. If we believe in principle that the Old and New Testaments are in agreement, then it follows that the New Testament must hold the same expectations regarding the futures of the wicked and the righteous.
8. The New Testament repeatedly uses words such as 'destroy' and 'perish' in regards to the wicked. Rather than redefine these words to mean the exact opposite of their common meaning, we should retain their literal sense. The plain and clearest meanings of these words point to the end of an individual's existence.
9. When Jesus warns that there will be 'weeping and gnashing' of teeth', it demonstrates that future judgment will

involve conscious suffering, but that does <u>not</u> mean that this suffering will be everlasting.

10. The Lake of Fire in Revelation is completely in line with all the warnings of destruction for the wicked. This it is also called the Second Death clearly points to a final end of an individual's existence and consciousness. Since the Old Testament regularly says that the wicked will be destroyed, and that Jesus taught that Gehenna was a place of fiery destruction, it follows that the Lake of Fire *IS* Gehenna, the place of final judgment.
11. The word 'eternal' (Greek *aionios*) has a much broader sense than just 'everlasting'. It refers to thoroughness and finality. When judgment is eternal, it doesn't mean that conscious suffering continues forever, but that the judgment will be utterly thorough and its effect is permanent. A further consideration is that the Greek word '*aionios*' can be literally rendered 'of the age', which quite nicely fits our This Age/Age to Come framework.
12. Contrary to popular sentiment which says that "Christians die and go to heaven", there is good reason to believe that instead, creation is renewed and restored to its uncorrupted state. The redeemed will spend eternity in this renewed, original creation. This fits the repeated promise throughout Scripture that the righteous shall inherit the land.

13. Jesus promised immortality, and apart from Him, the only thing in Scripture which had any bearing upon immortality was the Tree of Life. It is highly significant (and symbolic) that the only times that there is access to the Tree of Life is before the fall (Genesis 3), and after the purging of evil from creation (Revelation 22). Only those who are redeemed by Jesus can receive the gift of life from this Tree.

Epilogue: Tough Questions and Ramifications

Having completed this study, I realize that it seems to turn everything upside down. I said at the beginning that it took me years to have this change in thought, and still longer to be able to systematize it in an understandable way. Rather than rehash all the major points to firm up my argument (you can read the summaries of each part instead), I'd like to point out the deficiencies of standard Christian theology. The reason I do this is that I realize that when we get into our Christian circles, people simply are afraid to ask tough questions and challenge what's being said. So, I'll do it here.

TOUGH QUESTIONS

First, does it make sense that God would cut off access to the Tree of Life to prevent us from living forever, and then for us turn around and say that we have immortal souls and live forever anyway? Why do Christians insist that we have immortal souls when there is not a single verse in the Bible that says this is so, and, *repeatedly* says the opposite, i.e., that we die and lie in the ground for the worms?

Second, if being a Christian means dying and going to heaven, how come there is not one single verse that says so directly? Jesus and Paul *never* make a direct statement concerning this, and neither do the other New Testament writers.

Third, notice the amazing inconsistency of how we traditionally interpret John 3:16: *"For God so loved the world, that He gave His only begotten Son, that whoever believes in Him shall not perish, but have eternal life.* First, we say that perish means to live forever (only in an unhappy way), directly contradicting what perish means. Second, we say Jesus gives us eternal life, then turn around and say people have immortal souls and live forever anyway. Within one verse we directly contradict the key points: we are destined to perish, but Jesus will give us life instead.

Fourth, if we die and go to heaven, what is the promise of resurrection about? People often feel alarmed when I say we lie dead until the resurrection, and question how I got *that* out of the Bible; then when I ask "What do you do with the resurrection?" they respond, "That's when the souls are re-inserted into our bodies." *The Bible nowhere says such a thing,* and yet they believe that this is the Biblical truth. In reading 1 Corinthians 15, it is clear that that the Resurrection is the great centerpiece of Paul's theology; why is it taught so infrequently?

Fifth, if we die and go to heaven or hell, then why are we repeatedly warned of judgment day? If we go to our reward or punishment immediately upon death, isn't the judgment a moot point?

Sixth, if we die and go to heaven, why does Paul refer to the deceased as 'asleep'? Isn't that a strange way to talk about someone living in utter full abundance with Jesus?

I don't raise these questions to mock anyone; indeed, I was taught to believe these things. I raise them to illustrate how much we have to ignore the Bible in order to hold standard Christian beliefs. Repeatedly, I have shared some of the thoughts within this study, only to have a Christian ask me, "Where did you get *that?!*" I believe that I have demonstrated quite clearly that the Bible says something very different than what many of us were taught.

RAMIFICATIONS

I've offered up a major re-thinking of some critical areas of Christian thought. If you accept what I've presented here, and can see the Biblical logic of my arguments, then I'd like to flesh out a bit of the significance of it all.

First, if we do not have immortal souls, which I believe the Bible makes clear, then it follows that the only way a person can be tormented forever as punishment in the afterlife is by God *deliberately keeping them alive for the sole purpose of being tortured.* I do not believe the Bible teaches this about the afterlife, and it certainly doesn't describe God as being this malevolent.

The great punishment for the wicked is to lose the life that God offered to give them. When the unrighteous reject God, they reject life itself. I believe the weeping and gnashing of teeth that Jesus foretold is, in part, the reaction of people when they see what they could have had being offered to others but not to themselves.

Second, this being so, then we really need to be humble before God. To think that we have a life of our own as self-autonomous beings is really a heresy of the highest order. The serpent said to Eve, "You shall not die." He was saying "You don't need God." So leave it to Christian theology to repeat the serpent's boast! No, we are unbelievably, tragically mortal to the nth degree, and we'd better not forget it.

Third, if we realize how mortal we are, then we realize how utterly precious life really is. Scientifically speaking, it is ridiculously amazing that anything exists. The precise and specific requirements for the galaxies to exist and operate, for the placement of the planet earth at the right distance from the sun, the proper distance for other planets away from the earth, the delicate balance of chemicals and conditions on earth itself and myriads of other factors all point to a simple conclusion: *the odds are simply overwhelmingly against us being here.*

Add on top of that that life is a deliberate purposeful act of God, and that God deems it good is a holy statement of the highest order.

Fourth, if the soul and body are not separate compartments but actually a holistic unity (which is what the Jews thought), then it follows that there is no segregating the spiritual from the non-spiritual. The idea that a physical life is corrupt and impure is *not* a Christian or Jewish idea, but comes from the Gnostic teachings which the early church condemned.

The truly Biblical worldview is that the earth is the Lord's and all it contains. All of life is a sacrament of sorts, as none of it can be pried away from the soul. The soul is not separated from the body to purify it someday. The resurrection which is promised to us is the redemption of *all* of us, not just the better part or the worthy part (*there is no worthy part!*).

Fifth, if life was lost to us (in the Garden of Eden), and then will be available to us again in The Age to Come (The New Jerusalem), then we realize something very important; *The Entire Story of Humanity Is About Resurrection!* We have to get our thinking straight: the resurrection was not the reversal of the 'mistake' of Jesus' crucifixion; no, the cross was the doorway to the 'rightness' of resurrection.

Furthermore, the resurrection is not only about us living forever, though this is included; it is about the corruption of all creation being reversed. Right now, all of existence is broken; the resurrection of Jesus was the beginning of it being mended.

Sixth, if this world is our home after all as I've contended in these pages, then it means that of all people, Christians should be stewards of creation and seeking to nurture its well being, and not being advocates for its ruthless and senseless exploitation. Forests matter. The purity of water matters. The variety of animal species matters. Air pollution matters. Fetuses matter. The spiritual/physical divide is a false one; everything is physical and everything is spiritual for the Christian.

For I consider that the sufferings of this present time are not worthy to be compared with the glory that is to be revealed to us. For the anxious longing of the creation waits eagerly for the revealing of the children of God. Romans 8:18-19

He who testifies to these things says, "Yes, I am coming quickly." Amen. Come, Lord Jesus. The grace of the Lord Jesus be with all. Amen. Revelation 22:20-21

Appendix A: Comparison Chart of Pop & Biblical Theology

POP THEOLOGY	BIBLICAL THEOLOGY
1. We are sinful beings with immortal souls and mortal bodies.	1. We are sinful beings who are completely mortal, both body and soul.
2. Jesus died for our sins; if we accept Him, we will live forever in heaven; if we reject Him, we will live forever in hell.	2. Jesus died for our sins and to redeem creation. If we reject Him, we will be destroyed in the Lake of Fire. If we accept Him, we will

	live forever in the restored creation.
3. When Christians die, their souls go to heaven. When non-Christians die, they go to hell.	3. When Christians die, they are dead and await resurrection. When non-Christians die, they are dead and await resurrection.
4. Jesus will return. In this belief, there are various factors like the tribulation, the millennium, the rapture & Armageddon	4. Jesus will return. This return fulfills both the Old and New Testament concept of the Day of Yahweh / Day of Christ Jesus as a day of judgment and deliverance (for God's people).
5. Resurrection of God's people: Pop theology cannot accommodate this concep One weak idea is that	5. Resurrection of God's people: along with the Day of the Lord, which includes the return of Jesus, all the de-

the Resurrection is when souls are re-inserted into bodies, *a concept that has no Biblical support.*

ceased are brought to life for judgment.

6. Judgment Day/Day of the Lord/Day of Christ: *Pop theology has no way to logically incorporate this.*

6. Judgment Day/ Day of Christ: The wicked will be cast into the Lake of Fire which is the Second Death, thus fulfilling the Biblical warnings of perishing and destruction. The righteous will be given access to the Tree of Life, and thus receive immortality.

Appendix B: Scriptural Index

APPENDIX B: SCRIPTURE INDEX

APPENDIX B: SCRIPTURE INDEX

CPSIA information can be obtained at www.ICGtesting.com
261464BV00001B/1/P

9 781432 762322